SEMINAR STUDIES IN HISTORY

General Editor: Roger Lockyer

The Reign
of Mary I

Robert Tittler

Professor of History,
Concordia University

LONGMAN
London and New York

LONGMAN GROUP LIMITED
*Longman House, Burnt Mill, Harlow, Essex CM20 2JE, England
and Associated Companies throughout the world.*

Published in the United States of America
by Longman. Inc., New York

First published 1983
Second impression 1984
ISBN 0 582 35333 5

Set in 10/11 pt. Linotron Baskerville

*Printed in Malaysia
by Art Printing Works Sdn. Bhd., Kuala Lumpur.*

British Library Cataloguing in Publication Data

Tittler, Robert
    The reign of Mary I. – (Seminar studies in history)
    1. Great Britain – History – Mary I, 1553–1558
    I. Title   II. Series
    942.05′4   D347
    ISBN 0–582–35333–5

Library of Congress Cataloging in Publication Data

Tittler, Robert.
    The reign of Mary I.
    (Seminar studies in history)
    Bibliography: p.
    Includes index.
    1. Great Britain – History – Mary I, 1553–1558.
    2. Mary I, Queen of England, 1516–1558. I. Title.
    II. Series.
    DA347.T57   1983   942.05′4   82–23988
    ISBN 0 582–35333–5 (pbk.)

SEMINAR STUDIES IN HISTORY

The Reign of Mary I

SEMINAR STUDIES IN HISTORY

A full list of titles in the series
will be found on the back cover
of this book.

Contents

Contents

Seminar Studies in History

Founding Editor: Patrick Richardson

Introduction

The Seminar Studies series was conceived by Patrick Richardson, whose experience of teaching history persuaded him of the need for something more substantial than a textbook chapter but less formidable than the specialised full-length academic work. He was also convinced that such studies, although limited in length, should provide an up-to-date and authoritative introduction to the topic under discussion as well as a selection of relevant documents and a comprehensive bibliography.

Patrick Richardson died in 1979, but by that time the Seminar Studies series was firmly established, and it continues to fulfil the role he intended for it. This book, like others in the series, is therefore a living tribute to a gifted and original teacher.

Note on the System of References:
A bold number in round brackets (**5**) in the text refers the reader to the corresponding entry in the Bibliography section at the end of the book. A bold number in square brackets, preceded by 'doc.' [**doc. 6**] refers the reader to the corresponding items in the section of Documents, which follows the main text.

ROGER LOCKYER
General Editor

Acknowledgements

We are indebted to the following for permission to reproduce copyright material:

The British Library for an extract from ff. 27–28 *Harley Ms 444*; Catholic Record Society Publications for an extract from *Archdeacon Harpsfield's Visitation* 1557 edited by Rev. L. E. Whatmore pp 75–6 & 99 Vol 45, 1950 and pp. 188–89 Vol 46, 1951; The Folger Shakespeare Library for an extract from *X.d. 412*; The Controller, HMSO for an extract from the *Calendar of State Papers, Spanish, XIII* 1554–58 edited by R. Tyler pp. 293–94, 1950; The Huntington Library, USA for extracts from *The Copie of a Letter sent in to Scotlande* 1555 by John Elder STC 7552; Manchester University Press for an extract from 'The Book of Rates of 1558' from *A Tudor Book of Rates* edited by Prof. T. S. Willan pp. 8–9, 1962; Suffolk County Council Record Office for extracts from document Nos. EE2/E/3 ff. 26*v*. and 27*r*. *Eye Borough Records*.

Cover: Painting of Mary I by Antonio Moro. Reproduced by permission of the Mansell Collection.

Preface

The pages which follow are intended to convey to students of the Tudor period a summary of recent scholarship on one of the less familiar reigns. I have striven to avoid the clichés with which Mary's reign has often been condemned or defended, and to let the evidence speak for itself. I have also tried to show the student that the interpretation of our past is a continuing process, and have made extensive reference to successive interpretations of the subject. Finally, the book reflects the view that social and economic conditions and the flow of ideas are just as important in historical thinking as the reconstruction of political events.

Though I willingly accept total responsibility for whatever faults remain, I do so in the knowledge that several friends and colleagues, scholars all, have pulled me back from the edge of many more. My Concordia colleagues, John Ryan, Mary Vipond and Geoffrey Adams, helped me think through several chapters each. Dr Jennifer Loach generously and critically read nearly the entire manuscript. Dr J. W. Martin kindly permitted me to read and discuss several of his works in progress, and provided much inspiration by his perseverance and enthusiasm. Roger Lockyer proved a tireless and eagle-eyed editor, and Annabel Jones of Longman has been most supportive. Linda Bonin of Concordia University proved an able typist even at the busiest of times.

Robert Tittler, 1982

Part One: The Background

1   The Apprenticeship of Mary Tudor

For a future monarch, Mary had a most unusual and difficult start
in life, and one which tells us a great deal about English politics
in the first half of the sixteenth century. Born in February, 1516,
to Henry VIII and his first wife, Catherine of Aragon, Mary was
the heir apparent throughout her earliest years, and played the
normal role of a young princess at court. She was as close to both
her parents as the conventions of that age permitted. She received
a firm classical education, learned to play upon the virginals, and
faced the prospect of betrothal to scions of sundry ruling houses of
Europe. Yet the longer her father's desire for a male heir remained
unfulfilled, the more dissatisfied he became with his marriage, and
the golden days of Mary's childhood were soon over. In 1525 Henry
even considered giving precedence in the succession to his illegitimate son, Henry Fitzroy. Though he never actually carried this
out, Mary's future became increasingly uncertain. Admittedly, he
bestowed upon her the title of Princess of Wales in 1525, but he
also moved her from the court to her own household at Ludlow,
on the Welsh border. This proved a portentous separation.

Within two years the strains of the royal marriage became too
severe. In June, 1527, 'The King's Great Matter', Henry's efforts
to rid himself of an unwanted wife, became public knowledge, and
with it began the most trying years of Mary's life.

For the span of the divorce proceedings Mary endured in limbo.
Though still heir to the throne, she was clearly estranged from her
father and her future remained heavily clouded. When the collapse
of her parents' marriage reached its climax in 1531 Henry forbade
her further contact with her beloved mother. Two years later Henry
married his pregnant mistress Anne Boleyn and declared illegal his
previous marriage with Catherine. He also began the ruthless
process of downgrading Mary, the fruit of that first match.

During the next few years, in what should have been the prime
era of Mary's intellectual and personal development, she suffered
a sequence of humiliating degradations. Barred from further contact with Catherine and her Catholic entourage, stripped of much

of her household, deprived of her title and, finally, removed from the succession, Mary languished in both health and spirit. We read in ambassadors' reports of these years about her persistent fears of poisoning, frequent illnesses and occasional hysteria. Though Henry's attitude mollified considerably after his third marriage (to Jane Seymour in 1536) the damage had been done. Never again would her health be particularly sound, nor would she feel at ease with the English Protestantism of her father's instigation.

Oddly enough, the pressures on Mary began to ease after the birth of Edward to Queen Jane in 1537. She could more easily relinquish her rightful place in the succession to the long-anticipated male heir. She felt more comfortable at court in the years of Henry's marriage to Catherine Howard (August 1540–February 1542), whose family was more sympathetic to Catholicism, and she shared in the distinctly more mellow atmosphere which Henry's last wife, Catherine Parr, fostered in Henry's declining years. In 1544 Mary was reinstated in the succession by parliamentary statute (35 Hen. VIII c. 1), being placed between Edward and Anne Boleyn's daughter Elizabeth (see Genealogies, Table I). Henry's final will, made shortly before his death in 1547, further affirmed this arrangement.

At that time, Mary was not quite thirty-one years old. Thanks to Henry's last-minute generosity she could anticipate distinctly more bountiful circumstances than she had for some time endured. Throughout Edward's reign she enjoyed substantial estates, a full retinue, and at least some of the respect due to her as a princess: scant substitute for the fulfilment of marriage which she craved or for the peace of mind which still eluded her, but still a comfortable material situation. Though she got on well with Edward, she wisely remained away from the royal court. Such aloofness permitted her freedom from entanglement in court intrigue and, of greater personal importance, allowed her relief from the oppressive Protestantism which had become the dominant theme at court under the sway of Edward's uncle, the Duke of Somerset, Lord Protector of the Realm. In the privacy of her own household, Mary and her attendants were at first permitted to hold mass in the Catholic rite, and she became more than ever the symbol of traditional Catholic practice in Protestant England. The Emperor Charles V, her Habsburg cousin, staunchly defended her right to maintain this privilege, and numerous well-born English Catholics held no greater ambition than to serve her.

Yet after John Dudley, Earl of Warwick and shortly to be made Duke of Northumberland, succeeded Somerset as the effective ruler of England in 1550, Mary's situation deteriorated considerably. Here was a much more staunch and intolerant Protestant: one who saw Mary as the Habsburg foot in the English door, recognised her potential role as the leader of English Catholicism, and determined his policy accordingly. Before long Mary fought and ultimately lost a painful battle to keep the Catholic rite alive in her own household. At the peak of her subsequent despair she made efforts, ultimately unsuccessful, to flee abroad to Spain through the small Essex port of Maldon. By 1552, though her relations were still cordial with the young and frail King Edward, she had become most apprehensive about her future at the hands of Northumberland and the rest of the government in the event that Edward did not survive to maturity.

On the eve of her succession, therefore, Mary Tudor was in many ways old at thirty-seven, certainly embittered and otherwise fatally shaped by her peculiar apprenticeship. Not surprisingly, she would prove a distrustful Queen. Having been either rejected by or separated from those to whom she might normally have felt closest, she came to place her faith in ideals rather than in people. Chief among such ideals was her intense, non-intellectual, and wholly uncompromising devotion to Catholicism. Also considerably important was her desire to marry, and perhaps to know as a wife and mother that domestic felicity of which she had been deprived in her own adolescence. Finally, and obviously linked to these other considerations, came her preference for and trust in Spaniards, who had ever been her aid and comfort, rather than Englishmen. Thus equipped, Mary waited out what she must have suspected would be the final months of Edward's life, and did so without any certainty that she would, in the end, wear the crown.

2 The Condition of England

As the Princess Mary awaited her fate, the realm which she hoped to govern lay in the midst of profound economic and social changes, spanning the processes of manufacturing, commerce, and agricultural productivity and even the very size and structure of the English population.

The commercial backbone of England's economy had long been based on three chief activities: foreign trade (in which raw wool and woollen cloth were far and away the main exports), regional trade and the local commerce of the market town or fair. Beyond the exaction of revenue from tolls and customs, moreover, the central government interfered remarkably little in these activities (**68**). By the mid-sixteenth century, however, some of the fundamental features of all three types of enterprise were undergoing rapid change.

After the period of marked prosperity earlier in the century the woollen cloth industry faced sudden instability due to the saturation of accustomed continental markets. At the same time such traditional institutions as the gilds and even the chartered boroughs which acted to regulate economic activity came under heavy shelling from what we may now recognise as early capitalist free enterprise. In some areas, particularly in such older industrial cities as Coventry and York, manufacturers were moving out from the towns, where gild and corporate regulations were sometimes costly and oppressive, and into the countryside, where such regulations often did not exist (**49, 82**). In addition, the nature of some agricultural enterprises permitted husbandmen to start up ancillary manufacturing activities – especially in the textile trades – which also competed with the interests of the towns (**89**). The figure or the middleman, familiar in contemporary literature as the corn of wool 'bodger' (or sometimes 'brogger'), facilitated economic specialisation and furthered this growth of free enterprise (**10**).

In some areas the processing of foodstuffs and other consumer items had grown in scale, sometimes through technological innovations and sometimes through the expansion of credit mechanisms. Thus, for example, in the brewing industry the addition of hops to ale, resulting in true beer, allowed longer storage, wider distribution without spoilage, and larger scale production. In many areas ale-making, which had been a part-time, village-level industry, was giving way to competition from full-time and large-scale beer producers in central urban locations, much as present-day small shops may fall victim to supermarkets or chain stores (**100**).

These patterns of economic change not only threatened traditional craftsmen, merchants and gilds, but cut to the heart of medieval, pre-capitalist assumptions about the nature and purpose of production, employment and sales. Those assumptions were based upon the belief that the entire village or town community was a harmonious whole, in which the welfare of all the parts had to be served. That goal could only be achieved by maintaining the quality of manufactured products, regulating prices and wages and restricting competition by enforcing a system of apprenticeship. Only those who had served in the time-honoured fashion were permitted to take their place among the master craftmen or merchants. This system had been almost entirely self-regulating, with little interference from outside the community, much less from Westminster, considered either necessary or appropriate (**82**).

During a long period, of which Mary's reign was an important part, the traditional forms of pre-capitalist enterprise were giving way to those of early capitalism. One of the most frequently cited reasons for this profoundly significant change is the renewed growth of population which many consider to have been under way for at least a decade or two before Mary came to the throne (**27, 65**). This sustained population growth, probably first apparent in the countryside and small towns, stimulated consumer demand, drove up prices in the domestic market, and contributed to a steep rate of inflation. It had the additional effect of depressing wage rates and helping to create a reservoir of cheap and mobile labour, unwilling to serve lengthy apprenticeships before joining the work force. It also helped spawn the considerable problem of poverty and vagabondage which threatened to undermine the social stability which was a major concern of Tudor government (**29**).

Taken together, these developments provided sharp growing pains for the Tudor state, considerable instability for its economy, and a substantial challenge for its governors. The devaluation of the coinage begun by Henry VIII and resumed even more drastically under Edward VI, made the situation increasingly serious without doing as much to stimulate foreign trade as was once thought. Both towns and countryside were profoundly affected by the changes that were taking place. Many towns faced new economic and political challenges from the rising costs of repairing public works and replacing social institutions formerly run by the Catholic church, and from the rapidly growing numbers of indigent workers and migrants in their midst (**92**).

The countryside had to deal with the additional problem of what to grow and how to sell it. During the fifteenth century England experienced decades of dramatic expansion in the cloth industry without sustained increase of population; indeed, there were even occasional shortages of labour. Under these conditions the conversion of arable lands to pasture, often by process of enclosure, seemed to many a logical course. When cloth exports faltered in the late 1540s and early 1550s, a time of renewed population pressure and greater availability of labour, some farmers were encouraged to return pasture land to tillage. Others may have turned from raising sheep to raising cattle on the same pasture land, reacting to a probable rise in demand for beef. Still others turned to rural industries to supplement their earnings from agriculture (**29**). These conditions were not unique to Mary's reign, but they certainly were characteristic of it.

Ironically, one of the most dramatic social and economic factors of the time – and one which was *not* particularly characteristic of the rest of the century – may temporarily have relieved some of the population pressure at work in the mid-century, though it created serious problems of its own. Two successive harvest failures in 1555 and 1556 and epidemics of typhus and influenza between 1556 and 1558 combined to produce in Mary's reign the most intense demographic disaster of the century – only rivalled, if at all, by the plague and harvest failures of the 1590s. The mortality in these years has been estimated at one and a half times the normal rate (**69**, p. 127), while there is evidence of twice as many burials as usual in some four hundred parishes between 1557 and 1559 (**86**, p. 28).

As might be expected, this crisis seems especially to have hit the very old and the very young. Geographically, mortality was much higher in the towns, where greater congestion and poorer sanitation provided conditions in which disease spread rapidly. Typical of many was the borough of Tamworth, Staffordshire, where deaths averaged about forty a year throughout the century, but where ninety-five people were buried between March and December, 1557 (**81**, p. 58).

6

Thus, while all sixteenth (and especially mid-sixteenth) century English governments faced profound economic and social changes, Mary's regime would face additional serious problems, not of her own making, which were unique in degree to her reign.

Part Two: Analysis

3 The Accession of Mary Tudor

Flight and rally

The events which placed Mary on the throne in July, 1553, are less perfectly understood than perhaps any episode in the course of the English royal succession. Yet the success of Mary's forces in bringing about the near bloodless fall of a government which, however illegitimately conceived, had begun to function as a 'legal' entity, cannot simply be taken for granted.

Early in 1553 the health of the boy King Edward VI began to deteriorate, and the Duke of Northumberland, Lord President of the Council and effective ruler of the kingdom, arranged a May marriage between Lady Jane Grey – a legitimate but not the closest royal claimant – and his own son, Guildford Dudley. He then persuaded Edward to change the order of succession to the throne. By a document known as 'The Devise for the Succession' and by simple letters patent, it was now contrived that the throne should pass 'to the Lady Jane and her heirs male' rather than to Mary (see Genealogies, Table II).

In his effort to preserve his own power behind the throne, and with it the fervently Protestant regime which he had nurtured for three years, Northumberland seemed not to mind that such devices were legally incapable of overturning the 1544 Henrician Act of Succession (**36**). Mary, as he well knew, would not hesitate to restore a Catholic regime, and she would certainly not find a place in it for him or the rest of the Dudley clan. In view of these arrangements, it is surprising that Edward and Mary remained on friendly terms and that neither Northumberland himself nor the burning issue of religion severed the ties between them.

Once it became clear to him that Edward's days were indeed numbered, Northumberland played upon those ties and invited Mary to visit her ailing sibling, not letting her know just how grave matters had become. He hoped to have Mary arrested and out of harm's way before Edward died, thus aborting any campaign on her behalf.

As the young King breathed his last, on 6 July 1553, Mary had just reached Hoddesdon, Hertfordshire, *en route* to see him at Greenwich. Alerted in the afternoon to the actual state of affairs – which she may have anticipated to some extent – Mary recognised her peril at once. With only a token retinue, and uncertain of what efforts might be under way to capture her, she took flight immediately. Riding northward as swiftly as possible through dusk and then darkness, she appears to have travelled nearly 80 kilometres before coming to rest at the home of a Catholic gentleman, John Huddleston, at Sawston Hall, a few kilometres south of Cambridge. Here she spent the remaining hours of the night. She is said to have left in disguise early the next morning, accompanied only by one of Huddleston's servants, and made her way in a day and a half to her own Manor of Kenninghall, in Norfolk, a destination she had clearly contemplated from the start. Her choice was by no means random. Kenninghall was safely remote from Westminster, well favoured by a strong regional Catholic gentry and, should all else have failed, an easy distance from the port of Great Yarmouth and safety abroad.

Secure at least for the moment, Mary was not content to rest her saddle-sore body. For one of the few times in her career she displayed the decisiveness and courage which, in the end, saved her cause. On Sunday, 9 July, she began acting as Queen and never looked back, taking two steps of crucial significance on that day. First, she addressed to the Privy Council in London an assertion of her 'right and title' to the throne, with a laconic and courageous command that the council should attend to the formal proclamation of her title. Copies of that epistle, which still survive [**doc. 1**], were also sent to various towns and individuals. Second, she despatched a battery of letters to East Anglia and other parts of the realm to announce her accession and enjoin her loyal subjects to defend her. Some of these letters also survive, not only in the archives of East Anglian boroughs, but in towns as far distant as Chester.

The Privy Council, which was either still confident of Northumberland's strength or (as its members would later claim) too intimidated by his forceful presence, promptly rejected Mary's claims [**doc. 2**]. Yet the rapid circulation of news of Mary's flight, and perhaps the foreknowledge that she would attempt this strategy, had a telling effect outside Westminster. Supporters from various parts of the realm began rapidly to assemble, with gentry and their retainers and tenants arming and marching to Mary's defence

9

within a matter of a day or two. Indeed, one of the first recorded acts of Mary's government was to commission purveyors to supply her growing forces from the surrounding countryside of Norfolk and Suffolk.

The nature of this support has never been investigated satisfactorily, and indeed the scarcity of sources has made this a difficult task. But it seems likely that the 'Marian Rising' was prompted by more than mere Catholic sentiment or devotion to the Tudor dynasty, which are the accepted explanations (**50**, Ch. XI;**20**, Ch. 39). The common supposition that the rising largely involved East Anglia, while the rest of the realm waited to see what would happen (**16**, p. 259), also appears unjustified. One of the most sympathetic areas, for example, was a wide crescent-shaped band of hilly terrain roughly following the contours of the Chiltern Hills, including part of the Cotswolds as well, and taking in much of Berkshire, Oxfordshire, Buckinghamshire, Bedfordshire, Hertfordshire and Northamptonshire. Some of the earliest and most prominent of Mary's supporters held their chief lands in these areas, and several boroughs in the same region, including Aylesbury, Banbury, Higham Ferrars and High Wycombe, were later rewarded with charters of incorporation for their support at this crucial time (**92**).

As for East Anglia itself, many local gentry, Protestants as well as Catholics, undoubtedly did turn up with their tenants in Mary's camp, but here support for her cause was far from universal. The vital port of King's Lynn, for example, seems almost certainly to have been misled by Robert Dudley – another of Northumberland's sons and the future Earl of Leicester – into supporting Jane Grey well after it was prudent to have done so. Several members of the ruling oligarchy in Norfolk's other chief seaport, Great Yarmouth, were subsequently purged from office for supporting the Grey cause: evidence of that unfortunate choice has been firmly inked over in the Borough Assembly book, but can be read today with the aid of ultra-violet light. Though not strictly speaking an East Anglian borough, the Wash port of Boston had similar cause to seek the royal pardon once Mary was firmly established. Finally, there are clear indications of an anti-Marian rising in the Cambridge and Norfolk fenland, which seems to have endured even into August.

As might be expected, those who supported Mary came first from the gentlemen of her household and others, both Protestant and Catholic, from the region surrounding Kenninghall. In addition, a few peers, notably the Earls of Bath and Sussex, and some lesser officials from Westminster joined Mary's camp at Kenninghall. Yet even among such early enthusiasts motives were often more complex and personal than has generally been assumed. Events like Edward's death and the ensuing contest for the throne served to focus the sort of long-standing family and other rivalries which abounded in Tudor regional society. Thus, for example, it followed that when a Grey claimed the throne, his long-standing rivals, the Hastingses of Loughborough, would oppose that claim. When Thomas, Lord Dacre of Gilsland, supported Mary, Thomas, Lord Wharton, held back. When the aggressive grain merchant Osbert Mountford of Feltwell, Norfolk, supported Mary, his arch-rival Thomas Waters of King's Lynn, a sometime mayor and frequent MP, would not. In all these cases and many more besides the personal feud played as large a part as any dynastic principle in the determination of loyalty and commitment. As we are coming increasingly to recognise, this was the nature of Tudor political perceptions outside of Westminster, and ought not to surprise us.

Turning the tide

Gratified and reassured by the strength of this early response, Mary moved on 14 July, or thereabouts, to the more commodious facilities of Framlingham Castle in Suffolk. Within a day or two, and despite some continued opposition in isolated parts of the realm, this, too, filled with her supporters, and events rapidly turned her way. Jane Grey had been proclaimed at the Tower on the 10th but, though some courts did meet in her name and some regular business went on at Westminster, it rapidly became evident that Mary's forces would not be easily overcome. By the 13th Norwich and a few other towns had proclaimed Mary, and Northumberland had found it necessary to take personal command of an expedition to capture her. For him to have left London at this time was a most desperate act, but it obviously seemed to that seasoned commander a necessary risk in view of the situation. He thus set out with a small army toward Cambridge, and left his councillors to their own devices.

In his absence their support swayed, cracked, and finally tumbled down entirely. Sir William Cecil was commissioned by several of his colleagues to make a presentation of loyalty to Mary herself: a most courageous task! Though he carried it off successfully, it was to be his last significant political act prior to the accession of Elizabeth. Mary never trusted him to serve her, and never appointed him to high government office.

By 16 July Northumberland had reached Cambridge, hoping to approach Mary's gathering forces from the west and at the same time drive a wedge between her and the rest of the country. He had also sent a flotilla of six ships to cut off her potential retreat by sea through Great Yarmouth. But by the 18th several stalwart Marians, led by Sir Henry Jerningham, had effected a mutiny in the flotilla (3), and news of general disaffection toward the Dudley cause had begun to arrive from Westminster. Utterly discouraged, Northumberland fell back from near Bury St Edmunds to Cambridge. When Mary was officially proclaimed in London on the 19th, the point at which her reign is considered to have begun, he had no choice but to throw his cap in the air for her and hope for the best. Shortly thereafter he surrendered to a delegation led, ironically, by his councillor the Earl of Arundel. An ardent student of Tudor politics, Arundel had switched sides just in time.

From that point, Mary's march to the throne was all downhill. Within a few days she and her joyful entourage began its stately and triumphant procession southward, gathering well-wishers and hangers-on as it went. It passed through Colchester – where the Borough served up 59 gallons of claret and 3 tuns of beer[1] to smooth over any hint of earlier indiscretions – to Sir William Petre's home at Ingatestone, and on to London. Here, preceded by trumpets and drums and accompanied by thousands of followers, Mary entered on 3 August 1553.

Those who lined the streets and cheered the new Queen saw a frail but determined-looking woman, middling in height and fair of face, with auburn hair, high forehead and cheekbones, and brows made prominent by a myopic squint. Her voice, could they have heard it, was a resonant and even masculine contralto; her fortitude, could they have measured it, was considerable, and her desire to rule at last, intense.

The 'Marian Rising' had come to a successful end for the rightful heir, and with it, the brief royal career of Lady Jane Grey. Enjoying a remarkable degree of mercy from her victorious rival, Jane would not be executed until after Wyatt's Rising in the following year. Northumberland fared less well and was despatched within weeks. Yet even here Mary showed her mercy. The initial sentence had been for a traitor's death – the scaffold and dismemberment – but

[1] About 270 litres of claret and about 3,000 litres of beer.

she permitted him the honour of the block instead: a considerable courtesy, to the Tudor way of thinking.

Mary's accession and Mary's government

These dramatic weeks yielded more than a good story. The very circumstances of Mary's accession played a large part in the establishment and even the conduct of her government. Unlike her half-brother Edward, Mary had received little formal training for the tasks of government, and though she was certainly dutiful and earnest, neither her temperament nor her intelligence particularly helped her to master their complexities. More than most monarchs, Mary had – and, to her credit, recognised – a profound need for advice from those more able and experienced in affairs of state. But given the contentious circumstances of her accession and her own predisposition to distrust all but a select few, where could she turn? Nearly all of those with valuable experience at court had gained it in the service of her father or brother and, at least by implication, in the interests of the Reformation. Though she knew well enough whom she *could* trust, few of that small band of Catholic gentlemen had gained much useful experience during those Protestant regimes. The closest of them had served instead in her own household. Though some of these aides matured impressively in the years of her service, Mary knew better than to rely on them at the outset of her reign.

In consequence, the Marian regime consisted largely of men who fell into one of two categories: personal followers of staunch loyalty but slight experience, and men of stout experience and skill but of suspect and recent loyalty. Members of the former group – including Sir Robert Rochester, Sir Henry Bedingfield, Sir Francis Englefield and Sir Henry Jerningham – were in most cases members both of the royal household – where they enjoyed greater access to and potentially greater influence upon Mary – and of the Privy Council. Members of the second group – which included William Paget, Secretary Petre, Lord Treasurer Winchester and the Earls of Arundel, Shrewsbury and Pembroke – exercised a contrastingly formal relationship with Mary, but tended to hold more offices of state along with their membership of the council. Finally, and fortunately, there were a very few who shared both the Queen's trust and some experience at court. Chief among these was the forceful, conservative and highly influential Stephen Gardiner, Bishop of Winchester, whom she made her Chancellor (**93**).

Mary's government thus constituted a blend of new and old hands at court. It struggled both to maintain certain social and economic policies along the lines charted by its predecessors on the one hand, while striking out in very different directions in religion and foreign policy on the other. Not surprisingly, the opening years of the reign especially would demonstrate a great deal of political acquaintance-making among relative strangers, with the Queen herself very much a part of that process.

4 The Spanish Match

The succession problem and its possible solutions

The first weeks after Mary's triumphant arrival in London were devoted to the business of establishing her government after the collapse of what was now described as Northumberland's rebellion. The leaders of that failed effort were rounded up and placed on trial for their transgressions, though in the end relatively few were sentenced to the traitor's fate. The pardon rolls record for us the exoneration of the rest, as well as the names of many who simply wished to set straight the record of their loyalty and to enter the Marian era without taint of suspicion.

The Queen's coronation, held on the last day of September 1553, required a great deal of planning and activity, and effectively preoccupied many people at court for weeks beforehand [**doc. 3**]. Numerous rewards were distributed on that festive occasion to those who had supported Mary – many of them being announced on the occasion of the coronation – and the ranks of the royal household swelled accordingly.

There were, of course, matters which were not only pressing but of genuinely greater importance than the coronation for the new regime. These included the issues of religion and finance – both of which would necessitate the calling of parliament – and the related problems of the royal marriage and succession. Henry VIII's final will had specified that, barring issue from Mary, the crown would pass to Elizabeth. Feeling strongly about the perpetuation of a Catholic settlement, which Elizabeth could not be expected to uphold, and longing for a husband who might bring her some of the comforts of domesticity she so much desired, Mary determined to conclude a suitable marriage as soon as it could be arranged. Nearly all her advisers agreed. The only exception – and it was an ironic one, since he was a potential candidate himself – was Reginald Pole. Speaking from his Italian exile, he urged Mary to remain unwed, but no one took him seriously.

Of the few possible English candidates for Mary's hand the most likely was Edward Courtenay. His claim to eligibility rested on his lineage: as a great-grandson of Edward IV he was one of the last of the Plantagenets (see Genealogies, Table III). His father, the Marquis of Exeter, had been executed by Henry VIII, partly because of his closeness to the Princess Mary and his loyalty to the old faith. Courtenay himself had virtually been reared in prison since the age of twelve, a circumstance which evoked a good deal of sympathy from Mary. To his credit, he had used that time to cultivate his considerable intellect, but unfortunately he had had no chance to study men as well as books. This left him ludicrously ill-equipped to deal with the social amenities of court life. Though he was tall, handsome and learned, he was the butt of more than his fair share of jokes, and seemed unable to maintain the respect or even friendship of any but a few. One of those few, oddly enough, was the powerful Chancellor, Stephen Gardiner, who remained remarkably blind to the futility of Courtenay's candidacy.

Though Mary restored the Courtenay family to its inheritance and showered gifts and the earldom of Devon upon Sir Edward himself, this was probably more of an attempt to make him shine in the sight of other women than a true reflection of his image in her own eyes.

Failing Courtenay, the prospect of a foreign match became obvious, and there was no lack of potential suitors for such a prize as the Queen of England. Of the leading candidates, Prince Philip of Spain was easily the most prominent, though far from the most ardent. His lack of enthusiasm did not, however, deter his father, the Emperor Charles V, who saw the value of such a match for his plans, and let no obstacle stand in his path. Weary and ailing at fifty-three, Charles had already determined on his own abdication and on the division of his extensive territories between his son Philip and his brother Ferdinand. Philip would have Spain and the Netherlands, and Charles also considered it essential for him to gain England as a means of counter-balancing the rival power of Valois France. Furthermore, Charles longed to bring England back into the Catholic fold, and he was especially anxious that his own son should take the credit for that achievement (**58, 39**).

Negotiations for a Spanish match

After a good deal of diplomatic hide-and-seek Charles entrusted his ambassador Simon Renard with presenting to Mary an official proposal of marriage, which he did on 10 October 1553. Mary gave it deep thought, regrettably unbroken by much consultation with her advisers, and decided by the end of the month to accept the offer (**26**). In more than one way it was to be an unusual match. It was especially rare for an unmarried woman of royal birth to have a free hand in making her own marriage, and although Mary discussed the diplomatic implications at length with Renard, her choice was determined equally by her personal feelings. Philip, after all, represented most of those few things which Mary had come to trust and value: he was Spanish, Catholic, well-learned, experienced in affairs of state, and had a solicitous and most statesman-like father upon whom Mary had already relied for advice.

Though the final marriage treaty held considerable merit from the English point of view, the sudden prospect of a foreign Catholic monarch aroused in the realm an enormous reaction of xenophobia and indignation. Some – though far from all – of this must be blamed on the Queen herself. Having either failed to anticipate the strength of this reaction or decided not to bother about it, Mary demonstrated for neither the first nor the last time as monarch her failure at what we now call 'public relations'. The councillors as a group first learned of her decision on 8 November 1553, and though some had been prepared for the event by Renard – not by Mary herself – many even of the most prominent were caught by surprise. They might have realised at that point, if they had not already done so, that a certain gulf would always separate most of them from the Queen's confidence.

Gardiner had particular cause to be irked, for he had continued to support Courtenay long after Mary had ceased treating that prospect seriously; he thus looked very foolish indeed when Renard, not Mary, intimated to him the Queen's intentions toward Philip. Members of Mary's first parliament, then in session, were similarly distressed and when a delegation of their spokesmen, including several Privy Councillors, went to dissuade Mary on 16 November, she accused the Chancellor of putting them up to it. His rival William Paget, on the other hand, came out with head held high: he had been among the first to accept the prospect of Philip, and now had the perverse pleasure of watching Gardiner scramble to regain his esteem with the Queen (**93**).

Significantly, much of that scrambling, and the continued tension between Paget and Gardiner, contributed creatively to the business of writing the marriage agreement. Along with Renard, his aides, and Mary herself, the two councillors worked long and hard, and

17

in the end they helped produce and defend to their colleagues a treaty designed to allay English fears (**93**).

The terms of the ensuing agreement were accepted by the council on 7 December 1553, proclaimed five weeks later throughout the realm, and approved by Mary's second parliament in April, 1554 (1 Mary, st. 3, c. 2). Philip – who was not a direct party to these negotiations – was to receive the title of King but, except for what he would share with Mary as joint sovereign, he would gain nothing of the prerogatives, possessions or other perquisites which usually went with that title. England's laws were to be preserved in every respect, and no alien was to be permitted to hold English office. As for the succession, though the eldest surviving issue of Philip and Mary would inherit the realm of England, he or she too would be bound by its laws. If the marriage were to prove fruitless, or if Mary were to pre-decease her consort, he and his heirs would hold no further claim to the crown of England.

It was indeed unfortunate that Philip had not been involved in these negotiations, for he perceived in the treaty an extremely undignified settlement for one of his position. Though obliged to accept his father's decisions, Philip frankly avowed to his own aides his determination not to abide by any unwelcome restrictions placed upon him. This was not, of course, made known to the English, whose worst fears it would have confirmed.

Wyatt's Rising, January–February 1554

Even in ignorance of Philip's actual feelings and the circumstances surrounding them, English opposition was considerable. Though the Privy Councillors had no choice but to fall into line once Mary had made up her mind, the public outcry both in London and beyond rose quickly and resounded at length. A proclamation had to be issued enjoining restraint from 'unlawful and rebellious assemblies', and reports of 'lewd words', 'seditious tumults' and general disaffection poured into the court. More serious were the rumours of actual plots, involving Courtenay and the young Princess Elizabeth.

Such rumours were not unfounded. From the autumn of 1553 several influential gentry about the court – none of them councillors – began to discuss the prospect of engineering a Protestant succession. The logical means to this end was a marriage of Courtenay with Elizabeth and the deposition of Mary. As Mary's marital plans became more widely known these discussions in turn became more serious, and in December 1553 plans were concluded for co-ordinated risings in Kent, Hertfordshire, Devon and Leicestershire in the following spring. When the marriage treaty was signed on 12 January, and it became widely anticipated that the Prince himself would arrive toward spring, the conspirators were spurred to action. The date of the rising was set for 18 March 1554.

Unfortunately for the plotters, the government got wind of the plan in mid-January through Renard, and then the pathetic Courtenay was made to tell all he knew. Set at the last minute, three of the four tinder-heaps failed to ignite: Devon and Hertfordshire would not rise, and only a mere 150 men or so joined the Duke of Suffolk, father of Lady Jane Grey, before his effort sputtered out in the Midlands. The exception was Kent. Here Sir Thomas Wyatt, scion of a prominent shire family, rallied about him his tenants and other gentlemen of weight. These in turn succeeded in raising some 2,500 armed supporters, largely in the Medway Valley and such towns as Maidstone, Rochester, Tonbridge, Sevenoaks, and Cranbrook. Though others may have had their own motives for joining in, Wyatt's chief call was to English patriotism, and to an associated fear and resentment of the impending Spanish presence. Assured of support, or at least benevolent neutrality, from much of the northern and central parts of Kent, Wyatt seems to have envisaged a quick march on London where, with support from other parts of the realm, he could either compel Mary to disavow her plans for marriage or stage a coup to place Elizabeth on the throne.

Unaccountably, the government chose the Duke of Norfolk, a fine soldier in his prime but now in his ninth decade, to stop Wyatt's march from Rochester. How shocked they must all have been when, using words to greater effect than pikes or arrows, Wyatt's men caused Norfolk's forces to give way and persuaded many of them to join their ranks. By 29 January poor Norfolk had little choice but to return to court, and the way to London appeared to lie open to the rebels.

In these first anxious days of the rising the government experienced considerable difficulty in gaining reliable information and it remained uncertain how to react. Seen in retrospect, however, the Queen and council seem to have made all the right decisions after, if not before, the appointment of Norfolk. Not wanting to alarm the Emperor and not having much time anyway, they chose the tortoise's defence: they decided against calling for Imperial aid, fortified the capital, and prepared to wait out the foe on home ground.

Analysis

The choice proved astute in several ways. At this crucial juncture, when much of the realm lay waiting on events, the entrance of Imperial or Spanish troops would undoubtedly have played right into Wyatt's hands and fomented a general rising of 'patriotic' Englishmen. If the government had sent a second expedition into Kent, it would have taken the goalkeeper out of the goal, and left London open to attacks from other directions. Finally, the Queen knew that Wyatt's forces still had to cross the Thames to accomplish their purpose, and she placed great trust in her ability to rally the Londoners against them. When she made her public appeal Mary rose to her full powers, showing once again that splendid courage and fortitude which she had demonstrated at Edward's death. Addressing the citizens after Norfolk's shameful retreat, she lashed out at Wyatt as a wicked traitor, defended her religion and her choice of husband, and called on them 'as a mother doth love a child' to stand firm in her cause.

These tactical decisions, Mary's rare performance, and a crucial error by Wyatt proved just enough to win the day. Though handed the initiative by Norfolk's deserting troops, Wyatt unaccountably diverted his forces to take the militarily unimportant Cooling Castle, held by Lord Cobham, and thus did not reach the Thames at Southwark until 3 February 1554. By that time the Queen and her council had done their work, and London was prepared. After waiting three days in vain for the Londoners north of the river to rise to his cause, Wyatt grew desperate. On 6 February he led his troops some twelve miles west to Kingston, where he easily crossed to the north bank, and then marched back east an even longer distance at night to reach Kensington and the western edge of the city by dawn. Here, despite a degree of sympathy from some of the citizens, who were probably anxious to support the winning side whichever it might be, the rebels found their way blocked. Although they were less than two miles from the Tower and the Queen, they could not force their way through and they were compelled to lay down their arms and sue for mercy.

Much to its credit, the government proved as cool-headed in victory as in battle, for though Wyatt and some of his immediate supporters (as well as the innocent Lady Jane Grey, who was made to pay for her father's treason) were executed, the vast majority of his followers, especially among the rank and file, were set free. Even the Princess Elizabeth, an obvious element in Wyatt's plans whether she agreed with them or not, was merely placed in prison. The government was clearly determined not to play the vindictive role and not to justify the accusations of insensitivity to English interests which Wyatt's followers had cast at it. It may also be that the government was still uncertain of the extent of the rising or of its true motives, and hoped to avoid further antagonism in the months prior to Philip's arrival as the royal bridegroom.

According to the government version of the rising written by John Proctor (**4**), Wyatt and his cohorts objected most not to the Catholic restoration itself, but rather to the Spanish marriage. That view of the Rising allowed Mary and her councillors to continue in their avowed belief that the nation was still basically Catholic in sentiment, and to paint any opposition to Philip as an act of treason rather than of patriotism. Following Proctor's *Historie of Wyates rebellion* (1554) this approach to the episode has become an accepted tradition among most modern historians, being expounded most recently and at some length by Professor D. M. Loades (**39, 40**).

However, it now seems likely that the factors motivating Wyatt's followers were much more complex than has hitherto been assumed (**12, 90**). For one thing, while some leading Kentish Protestant interests remained conspicuously loyal to the crown, a considerable number, including a majority of the most radical, flocked to Wyatt's camp. The borough of Maidstone, for example, which would lose more Protestants to later Marian religious persecution than any other borough in the shire, was Wyatt's first and greatest urban stronghold. It strains credibility to claim that such fervent Protestant support came to Wyatt with no other intent than to oppose the Spanish match.

Secondly, it is also clear that Kent as a whole had experienced a precipitous and very troubling decline in its cloth industry; had a tradition of popular protest both of long-standing duration and frequent expression; and had recently undergone a considerable shake-up in office-holding among the gentry who comprised its governing structure.

These factors suggest that those who followed Wyatt did so for a variety of reasons, of which a call to a secularly conceived English patriotism in opposition to the Spanish match was but one. Some people, including Wyatt himself, no doubt feared a Spanish take-over of government and foresaw the possibility that considerable sums of English money would have to be spent on the defence of Spanish interests abroad. But others were clearly Protestant die-hards for whom the Spanish match merely added insult to injury. Some gentry probably saw the episode as an opportunity to regain lost ground in the eternal contest of shire politics. At least some yeomen, husbandmen and urban workers saw in Wyatt a vehicle for the expression of social and economic grievances, while others simply followed their landlords and employers. These factors not only belie the narrowness of the traditional explanation. They also demonstrate the importance of regarding 'official' explanations, however enshrined in historiographic tradition, with a certain caution, and of looking beyond the narrow confines of Westminster to the country as a whole in the effort to interpret national events.

The royal marriage

Whatever we may make of Wyatt's Rising at four centuries' distance, it is not surprising that the Imperial ambassador, Renard, and thus Philip and Charles, should have interpreted it as a public reaction against the impending Spanish marriage. Even after the ratification of the treaty itself, Philip was therefore more reluctant than ever to sail for England.

The apprehensive Queen can hardly have been reassured by the vagueness surrounding Philip's plans. Though some observers expected him to arrive as early as February, 1554, Philip managed to put off any decision until mid-July. Meanwhile there was complete uncertainty in England not only about the time of his arrival but also by what route and with what entourage he would travel and for how long he would stay. The English court made countless preparations, which were then delayed and finally abandoned or further postponed. An English retinue of well over three hundred persons, including a complete household and bodyguard, was established by mid-May, but then sat in humiliating idleness.

Mary herself endured the chagrin of travelling to the market town of Bishop's Waltham, near Southampton, and waiting for nearly a month before her betrothed actually sailed into view. Eventually, however, Philip did arrive, and in a carefully staged reception he met Mary at Winchester for the first time on 23 July 1554. To everyone's dismay he came fully accompanied by his own large retinue, making redundant many of the English preparations so long concluded and disappointing a bevy of young English gentlemen who had hoped to find a place in the Prince's following. By some remarkably foreboding coincidence, Philip's first days on English soil were met with dreary weather and incessant downpours (**50, 39**).

The marriage of Mary and Philip took place at Winchester on 25 July 1554 [**doc. 4**], and the royal couple, who shared no common spoken language, settled in to an uneasy spell of making each other's acquaintance. Though Philip was by all accounts admirably gracious to everyone, within a month of his arrival he had arranged for a ship to lie ready for his return voyage to Spain.

Philip may well have been extremely puzzled by the continued English chilliness toward him, a reserve which he could hardly have failed to perceive even in his sheltered surroundings. To his credit in that uncomfortable situation he made continual, lavish, and extended efforts to earn the regard of his new subjects, but the problems were not entirely of his own making or within his power to dispel. Though some cause for resentment may have lingered from the souring of Anglo-Spanish relations in Henry VIII's day, other and more profound factors were also at work. The first was the geographical isolation and relative cultural insularity of mid-sixteenth-century England. Foreigners were still rare enough to be conspicuous and, as the infamous London May Day Riots of 1517 had shown, were often bitterly resented. This was all the more true in the London region, where both the greater concentration of foreigners and the economic competition they provided had been most keenly resented. But the dislike felt for Philip did not derive simply from the fact that he was a foreigner. He had managed, by the age of twenty-six, to acquire a nasty reputation among his Dutch subjects which was entirely familiar in English political and commercial circles. He represented Catholic rule at its harshest and most uncompromising, and although he made a point of drinking English beer and doing his best to adapt to English customs, he personified to many Englishmen what has been termed the 'black legend': a particularly vivid stigma attached to Spain and the Spaniards both in England and elsewhere in the sixteenth century (**43**).

This underlying hostility was most symbolically expressed by parliament's insistence that Philip should not be formally crowned – a deprivation that deeply offended the ceremonious Spanish, and especially Philip. It is little wonder that when all this was added to his deep and genuine entanglements in continental politics, Philip did not spend any more time in England than was strictly necessary during his nominal reign as King. Yet his kingship, however perfunctory and short-lived, was not without its influence in English affairs, and not all of that influence was as perverse as has often been asserted.

23

5   Religion: the Catholic Restoration

Introduction

It was anticipated by all, in July, 1553, that Mary as Queen would continue in that faith which no intimidation had led her to give up as Princess. Yet it was far from clear what form a Catholic restoration would take or how rapidly it would come about. The uncertainty surrounding these issues extended to Mary's councillors as well as her subjects, and many were genuinely surprised and disappointed when she revealed her intention of restoring papal supremacy. In truth, Mary herself was as unknown to her subjects as they to her, a fact which she unfortunately never quite perceived.

Professor Loades's recent description of religious feelings at Mary's accession – 'frequent enthusiasm, occasional resistance, and a large amount of unchronicled indifference' – is as apt as one is likely to find (**39**, p. 153). For her part, Mary merely assumed that the majority of her subjects were still fundamentally Roman Catholic and had been led astray by a minority which had previously enjoyed government support. In her myopic view, the true Protestants were not only a minority, but were themselves dominated by a hard core of desperate and determined heretics, bent on perpetuating the grip of Satan upon the rest. It followed from this that a restoration of the Catholic faith would require little more than the removal of these hard-liners and a comprehensive provision of opportunity for resumed Catholic practice. As events would show, these convictions were as dangerous as they were erroneous, yet they coloured almost every aspect of her attitude towards the church now in her care.

The early weeks of the reign yielded little sign of the intensity or narrowness of the Queen's vision. An early proclamation gave assurance that she 'mindeth not to compel any her said subjects thereunto [religious conformity] until such time as further order by common assent may be taken therein', but this was intended to serve only until the details of her programme could be worked out. During these same weeks many of the most prominent Protestants were deprived of their livings, and some – including Thomas Becon, Thomas Cranmer, John Hooper, John Rogers, Hugh Latimer and Nicholas Ridley – were imprisoned. Virtually all of the printers who held patents under Edward were deprived of them and thus in most cases lost their livelihood. Foreign Protestants were at first encouraged and eventually ordered to leave the realm. A modest exodus then ensued from the universities, especially Oxford, and from the refugee communities, such as that led by John á Lasco, which had sprung up in the cordial atmosphere of Edward's reign. Six bishops and the Archbishop of York were deprived of their sees, four of them for having married. Yet none of these steps revealed a great deal about Mary's plans for religious change. Most people waited, sensibly enough, for the first meeting of parliament to see just how the wind would blow, and how strongly.

First steps toward Catholic restoration, 1553

Even in that parliament, which met in October, 1553, the government's programme seemed moderate enough, as Mary still lingered under the expectation of a large-scale and voluntary resumption of Catholic practice. Her first parliament repealed ecclesiastical legislation of Edward VI's reign, and restored the service in use at Henry VIII's death. It also imposed sanctions against those who interfered with the work of the clergy, or who abused the Catholic rite, and it implicitly reaffirmed the traditional doctrine of the Lord's Supper. Despite the importance of the royal supremacy in the Queen's mind, parliament was not asked to annul it. Though the passage of these provisions must have pleased the government well enough, members of parliament made it known that they would not automatically approve of all the demands that were put before them: they declined to proceed with a bill punishing those failing to attend church services and, in their first defence of lay ownership of clerical lands, they refused to revive at this time the bishopric of Durham which had been abolished in the previous reign (**39**).

During these same weeks Mary turned to the material and practical condition of her church, and began well-intentioned, if inadequate, work to build up both its clergy and its finances. The substantial majority of clergymen in July, 1553, were unprepared either by training or inclination to bear the burdens of a Catholic restoration, but Mary may have done more harm than good by depriving around twenty-five per cent of them of their livings, perhaps as many as two thousand clerics in all: most of them for having abandoned their celibacy and taken wives. Although many such clerics eventually gave up their wives and were reinstated, these deprivations did a great deal to aggravate the already serious short-age of manpower in the Church (**85**), but it never occurred to Mary to delay or to compromise on what was for her an entirely immoral Protestant innovation.

In a variety of other measures she and her bishops encouraged greater diligence in clerical performance; with preaching, pastoral care, and more regular lay attendance at services [**doc. 5**]. Though she should have been alerted to the general sensitivity regarding the lay possession of former church lands, Mary still hoped for a while longer that a widespread and voluntary return of church lands might ensue. In order to set an example from above in this regard she began herself to restore certain lands which remained in crown hands. Thus, she managed to refound a few monastic institutions in the London area, including Westminster Abbey, and she contributed on an *ad hoc* basis to relieve the short-term financial crisis of several dioceses. Toward the same end she restored First Fruits and Tenths[1] to the secular clergy in 1555 (**84, 75**). Yet while these measures deprived the crown of revenues upon which it had come to depend, they neither prompted the hoped-for lay response nor had much long-term effect on the desperate financial situation of the church.

The restoration defined, 1554

The year 1554 must be deemed pivotal in the effort toward Catholic restoration. It began with Mary's growing realisation that she had underestimated the staying power of her Protestant opponents; it spanned the coming of Philip and the return of Reginald Pole to England's shores; and it marked the peak of parliamentary efforts to restore a Catholic regime.

With the scare of Wyatt's Rising in the beginning of the year, and the more enduring background noise of discontent at both the Spanish match and the strengthened Catholicism which it foretold, Mary rapidly lost most of her initial naivety and began visibly to

[1] First Fruits: the first year's income of an ecclesiastical benefice, formerly paid to the bishop by the new incumbent.
Tenths: A tenth part of the same income, formerly paid to the Pope. Following the Henrician reforms both had been paid to the Crown.

stiffen her stance. While on the one hand a number of lay opponents were executed in the aftermath of Wyatt's Rising, Mary also set out to discredit the most devious leaders of England's Protestants. Beginning in April, 1554, Cranmer, Ridley and Latimer, already deprived of their posts and lingering in prison, were made to take part at Oxford in a public disputation with the flower of Catholic divines drawn from the universities. The government intended to ridicule and humiliate these leaders, but was not entirely successful – although when faced with death almost two years later in March, 1556, Cranmer took back a great deal of what he had earlier defended. In the disputation itself, Ridley especially – though deprived of books, papers and counsel – stuck fast and brilliantly to his views. The Oxford disputations did not mark in a chronological sense the beginning of the Marian persecutions, for the Protestant trio exhibited on that occasion were allowed to linger for more than a year before being dispatched as heretics, but they did provide an unmistakable and chilling portent of increasing ruthlessness on the government's part (**38**).

In July, 1554, Mary concluded her explosively controversial marriage with Philip, and it could hardly have escaped the government's attention that the Protestant cause, spurred on by the apparent affront to national pride of the Spanish match and left speechless by the failure of the Wyatt episode, was never more active. Though they may have been weakened in the short run by the hundreds who fled abroad, Protestants in many parts of the realm continued to be served by a flourishing underground of preachers, organisers, and literature smuggled in from abroad.

There is still much to be discovered – if indeed it ever can be – about these courageous non-conformists, but it is evident that they continued to use the Prayer Book of 1552 and otherwise kept alive as best they could the practices of the Edwardian church. Some of the actual congregations are noted in government reports or trials, and others through correspondence or recollections of their members. These must have been only a part of a larger movement of which record, understandably, has not survived. The vast majority of Protestant sympathisers in Mary's reign probably did not stick their necks out to the extent of joining an underground congregation, and only a very small percentage – nearly all of them relatively well off – fled abroad. The majority conformed outwardly to some degree or other in the hope of a more congenial settlement, for as long as Mary remained childless they had good reason for hope. For its own part, Mary's government reacted more directly to the zealotry of a few than to the general dissatisfaction of the many.

The role of the Spanish

In this increasingly hostile atmosphere, Mary looked for help from others, and found it both in Philip's entourage and in Reginald Pole. From the very first weeks of her reign she had looked to the Emperor Charles for advice on how to proceed, and in fact on some issues she consulted him and his ambassador Simon Renard even before her own councillors (**26**). When Philip came to England in the summer of 1554, on what for him and his father was in large measure a mission with ecclesiastical overtones, it was only natural that Mary looked to him in the same way. Philip was well prepared for that prospect. He had either brought with him or would shortly be joined by a coterie of forthright, outspoken, and conservative Spanish clergy, and although little is yet known about their precise activities, it is difficult to imagine that their role was entirely ceremonial.

At least three of these Spanish clerics were Dominicans: members of an order which was more prominent than any other in defence of the late medieval church against reform from within and attack from without. In the person of Girolamo Savonarola the Dominicans had run a puritanical reign of terror in Florence. In the person of Jacob Pfefferkorn they had led the campaign against Johannes Reuchlin, Ulrich von Hutten, Erasmus, and other Christian Humanists; in the person of Johann Tetzel and Johann Eck they first challenged the young Luther. Now they threatened to bring their counter-reformation vigour to England to combat the native form of heresy in that realm.

One of the three Dominicans, Juan de Villagarcia, was appointed by Pole to a divinity chair at Oxford, and took considerable credit for securing Cranmer's recantation (**57**, III, i, 475 and ii, 29). Another, Fr Pedro de Soto, had been Charles's own confessor, and was sufficiently trusted by Reginald Pole to be employed in interceding with Charles to permit Pole's return to England. Ironically, de Soto reached England before Pole, and the Cardinal later appointed him as Villagarcia's successor in the chair in divinity at Oxford. The third Dominican, Bartolome Carranza, later bishop of Toledo, was well known for his writings in defence of the Church, and came to serve as Mary's own confessor. There was, in addition, the Bishop of Cuenca, Alfonso de Castro, a Friar Observant, who was one of the Church's acknowledged authorities on the theory and practice of persecuting heretics, and the author of several works on the subject. De Castro accompanied Philip to England for his wedding, heard his confession, offered mass in his presence the day after, and urged him to more zealous persecution of heresy in England in 1556 (**38**). True, like the rest of the Spanish entourage, these men were precluded from holding government office and are not often cited in the state papers of that time, but they can hardly have been bystanders to the increasing intolerance emanating from Westminster after 1555. If we can believe John Jewel's 1559 comment on the work of de Villagarcia and de Soto at Oxford, 'one could scarce believe that so much mischief could have been done in such a short time' (*Cal. State Papers, Foreign, 1558–9*, 269–70).

Reginald Pole

Mary's other chief source of support and counsel in religious affairs was, of course, Reginald Pole, about whose activities much more is known for certain. Right from the time of Mary's accession, Pole had made strenuous efforts to end his continental exile of over two decades so that he could bring his talents to bear on a Catholic restoration in England. Those talents were considerable. Pole, whose household had been an important centre for English students in Padua in the 1520s, returned briefly to England in 1529. Unable to accept the break with Rome which was then under way, however, he returned to Padua in 1532, resisting first the King's entreaties and then his commands to return. At Padua he augmented his already sound reputation as a Christian humanist and advocate of reform in the Church, and became close to such eminent progressives as Gasper Contarini, Jacopo Sadoleto and Ludovico Beccadelli. At the request of Paul III he worked from 1536 on the report known as the *Consilium delectorum Cardinalium . . . de emendenda ecclesia* which served as the basis of the decision to convene the Council of Trent (1545–1563). In the process, he became a cardinal, though not yet a priest, and gained a reputation as one of the Church's authorities on pastoral care and clerical education, and one of its most respected diplomats (**55, 21**).

Although Mary came to the throne in July, 1553, Pole did not arrive in the realm until November, 1554. Ironically, he was not only kept away through the insistence of Charles V, who wanted

Philip to become established in England before Pole's return, but also by Mary herself. Having been away from England for over two decades – and two most eventful decades at that – it was hardly to be expected that he would have remained in touch with English sympathies or political realities. This was made abundantly clear in the letters he wrote to the Queen prior to his return. Mary was also aware that when Pole did return, he would do so as cardinal legate – an office accorded him by the Pope in October 1553 – and with the official assignment of reconciling England to the Papal See. While Mary clearly longed for such a reconciliation, she knew enough about the attitudes of her subjects to fear the prime condition attached to it: the restoration to the Church of all lands which had been taken from it since Henry's break with Rome. In view of the resistance which this demand could be expected to provoke, Pole's return would have to be delayed until she felt herself to be in a position of sufficient strength to dissuade him from insisting on this provision. Therefore, though she consulted him frequently after her accession to the throne, and was not concerned simply to assuage his bewilderment and disappointment at seeing his exile prolonged, she actually worked to delay his arrival. Philip, who wished to gain as much credit as he could for bringing about ecclesiastical change in England, gladly concurred.

Reconciliation with Rome

By the end of the summer, with the marriage concluded and Philip strong beside her, Mary turned to the next stages in her planned restoration of the Catholic faith. These involved an autumn or early winter parliament which could last complete the basis for the restored Church, and also grasp the prickly nettle of papal supremacy. This issue, of course, could not be handled without the acquiescence of the Papacy itself, and that meant dealing through Pole. With Mary's full support, it was Philip who, while trying as delicately as possible to soften the Cardinal's uncompromising attitude on the need to return former church lands, took the lead in arranging for Pole's return to his homeland as papal legate.

When Parliament convened on 12 November 1554, the government had in readiness for its consideration what amounted to the second half of the programme to restore Catholicism. The centrepiece of that effort was to be the arrival and participation of Pole himself, and a proclamation issued two days prior to Parliament's sitting enjoined obedience to him in his full legatine capacity. After an eleven-day journey, in which he was escorted by numerous English worthies sent to meet him, Pole reached Westminster on 24 November. Not only had all ceremonial niceties been extended for his triumphant return, but parliament did its work too. Though the two Houses did not consider the religious settlement as such before his arrival, they speedily repealed the act of attainder which had hung over Pole's head since the reign of Henry (31 Henry VIII, c. 15), and Philip and Mary took the unaccustomed step of journeying to the Lords' Chamber to assent to that bill on the 22nd.

Six days later the King and Queen summoned members of both Houses to the court to hear Pole deliver his offer of reconciliation [**doc. 6**]. In essence, he presented his Papal mandate to grant absolution and reconciliation of the realm of England with the Papal See in return for the abolition of all ecclesiastical legislation passed since 1529, including the Act of Supremacy. The one exception to this wholesale repeal was legislation confirming the confiscation of church lands. Though Philip and Mary softened Pole's stand somewhat, the question of a dispensation permitting holders of former church lands to retain them lawfully was left for later consideration. Meanwhile, both Houses of parliament spent three weeks working together, through the device of a special joint committee, to draft a bill of supplication to the King and Queen in which they accepted Pole's terms and agreed to the restored supremacy of the Pope, but left the property issue unresolved.

One of the most dramatic and emotion-charged days of the entire reign ensued on 30 November when, in a ceremony filled with pomp and joy, Pole welcomed in the Pope's name 'the return of the lost sheep' and granted absolution to the whole realm. Within days of this triumph for Mary's plans the negotiations for the land settlement began in earnest, and this proved a more drawn-out affair. In the end, in January 1555, Pole reluctantly agreed to concede lay ownership of church lands redistributed after the dissolution of the monasteries and other foundations under Henry VIII and Edward VI. The ensuing bill received the royal assent on 16 January.

Pole's strategy

From the moment of this dramatic reconciliation, and with the blessings of Philip and the relief of Mary, Pole assumed charge of the restoration effort. Despite his unfamiliarity with the state of the realm – a shortcoming which Mary and her councillors tried assiduously to overcome – Pole was in many ways particularly well-suited to the task. In addition to his vast experience with the workings of the Roman Church, he was well respected in the realm and skilled in the business of organisation which was now so much in demand. However, he still bore some handicaps, and never quite acquired the necessary perspective on the problem of restoration. Though he understood the power of the written word sufficiently to censor the attacks of his opponents, he failed to answer them in kind or to motivate others to do so. Though he directed his bishops and clergy with the utmost foresight and efficiency, he failed to inspire them. Though he understood well enough at least some of the apathy and disaffection of the general public, he preferred to work with the clergy rather than the laity. Finally, while his own Englishness led him in part to reject the proffered help of the Jesuits in 1555, it failed him when it came to understanding the cultural pride of his fellow-countrymen and their subsequent coolness to what many of them continued to regard as a foreign church.

For better or for worse, Pole thus set forth to do battle with a twenty-year legacy of spiritual waywardness, material decay [**doc. 7**] and clerical ignorance and disaffection. He rapidly identified financial impoverishment and the lack of ecclesiastical discipline as his chief priorities, and chose to put off working directly with the laity until he had restored sound discipline and management in the clerical hierarchy. He intended to rebuild from the top downwards, taking his time as he did so, and he therefore rejected such short-term potential panaceas as preaching and evangelism, which the Jesuits offered to provide. In the end this turned out to be a mistaken strategy, for neither Pole nor his Queen lived to see the fruit of such long-term plans, and the spirit of Catholicism in the Elizabethan age would owe little to his efforts. Pole was not to know this, however, and once he had mapped out his path he went to work with a vengeance. (**83**).

The business of restoring financial solvency and good management makes dull reading, but most of Pole's positive achievements lay in those areas. Beginning with his important London Synod of 1555, Pole sent his troops into battle first as administrators and pastors and only secondly as preachers. Emphasising the need for leadership before the role of the laity, he enjoined the bishops to take stock of their dioceses in regular visitations, and to institute regular auditing of diocesan and parochial finances. He urged them to set examples of regularity and discipline for their clergy, and he deserves credit for shaping a youthful but determined and highly qualified episcopate – only one member of which, significantly, would be swept along with the Protestant tide at the accession of Elizabeth. As for the clergy themselves, he did what he could to keep them up to the mark, though the numerous impediments to his ideals forced him to make concessions.

The Twelve Decrees which were drawn up by the Synod of 1555 included stern admonitions on the need for every parish priest to be resident, but despite a substantial number of recruits to holy orders, the still terrible shortage of qualified clergy necessitated over two hundred dispensations for pluralism. Though Edwardian ordinations were generally not accepted, Pole was compelled to recognise those who had entered orders between 1532 and 1547: there were simply too few qualified clergy on hand to have done otherwise. To help these undermanned legions in their work, Pole commissioned a newly edited Catholic New Testament, a new Book of Homilies – especially useful to hard-pressed clergy – and a new catechism, but these never had a chance to be implemented (**85**).

Finally, Pole brought with him from his continental reformist experience a deep concern for clerical education: a concern which (though Pole would not live to see it) resulted in one of the few distinct victories for the reformers in the Council of Trent. Pole exercised his concern for education in two capacities. As cardinal legate he encouraged frequent parochial visitations in which his bishops were to report on the state of learning in the dioceses among the schoolmasters as well as the clergy, and he called for the establishment of seminaries in each diocese of the realm. Secondly, in 1556 he was named to succeed the deceased Gardiner as Chancellor of Cambridge and, later on, of Oxford. He thus represented the chief link between the government and the universities. Here again he placed great emphasis on visitation, naming the Padua-trained humanist and civil lawyer Nicholas Ormenetti as Visitor to the universities in 1556. He also hoped to shore up the teaching of divinity, and he did much to create the climate of opinion which led to the founding of two new Oxford colleges, Trinity and St John's, by private individuals. Yet the government's hopes for lay refoundation of grammar schools, primed by the founding or refounding of five by the Queen herself, met with little response in the short period of the reign (**85, 64**).

This, then, is the positive side of Pole's reform programme and, given time, it might well have produced the sort of sound Catholic church which could have endured on a permanent basis. However, the premature deaths of Mary and Pole left the Protestant tide to wash over, once and for all, what turned out to be castles in the sand.

The persecution of the Protestants

What one chiefly remembers of the Marian church today, of course, is the other side of the coin: so much so that the most recent scholarly biography of the Queen is entitled *Bloody Mary* (**20**). Once parliament had revived the treason legislation of the Middle Ages the way lay open to prosecute heresy on a wide front. The government, with the Queen very much at its head in this regard, lost little time in so doing. This effort actually proceeded on two fronts, as Pole took particular care to suppress seditious writings as well as seditious Protestants, but it is the latter that has had much the greater impact on the English popular imagination.

Between February 1555 and the end of Mary's reign the government executed for heresy just under three hundred Protestant nonconformists. Nearly all of these were burned publicly for heresy, and provided the occasion for widespread popular witness and sympathetic Protestant reaction. Though a few of these were the sort of true radicals – Anabaptists, Lollards, or others – who would have met a similar fate under any English regime, most were Edwardian Protestants who were either unwilling to accept the Catholic view of the Eucharist, or who demonstrably refused to conform to the restored Catholic rite.

The identity of the victims and the sequence in which they suffered their fates has also been particularly important in the creation of the tradition of the Marian Martyrs. As it happened, a very large proportion of the earliest victims were popular preachers of considerable stature. The horrible and public execution of John Rogers at Smithfield (4 February 1555) or of the extremely popular Rowland Taylor at Hadleigh, Suffolk (9 February 1555) had enormous emotional impact and wide notoriety. The popular sympathy evoked by those early burnings, marked by frequent popular demonstrations, completely undermined any possibility of discrediting Protestants as the government sought to do (**1**) [**doc. 8**].

The later victims, and by far the majority of the total number, were men of humbler status, almost all of them artisans, labourers, yeomen or husbandmen. It seems a justifiable assumption that they stuck to their views to the point of martyrdom through the strengthening example of their 'betters' who went before them. Their own fortitude, in turn, strengthened the will of their equals, who formed part of the very fabric of English society. The effect of the martyr-doms as a whole served not merely to undermine the government's efforts at uniformity, but also to confirm in the faithful that they indeed were God's chosen if they retained their courage under such duress.

However great the enormity of persecution may strike us today, historians of the Continental Reformation may well be puzzled by the great attention which the Marian martyrs have always received in the literature of English history: some two hundred and ninety martyrs in four years seems a small number compared with the thousands slaughtered in the name of some version of the 'true faith' in nearly all other parts of Europe, including Scotland, in the same century. The English themselves certainly accepted corporal punishment – including burning for the crime of heresy – as quite a normal penalty, and often flocked to witness such occasions. Yet measured in the quantity of ink poured out through the centuries to describe, condemn or even defend this Marian experience, the evidence speaks for itself (**25**).

There would appear to be several explanations for this conun-drum. It has been argued, for example, that England was less accustomed to the sort of violence to which, in the guise of frequent warfare, most Europeans of this age had become somewhat inured. Again, there was the element of foreign intervention in the English martyrdoms. Although the extent of Spanish influence is in fact altogether uncertain in most aspects of Mary's reign, Spain above all nations had acquired a contemporary reputation for cruelty (**43**), and the Spanish marriage coincided with the emerging Eng-lish self-identity characteristic of the Tudor era. Finally, at the end of the day, it was the victors who wrote the 'received' version of events, and the Protestant regime of Elizabeth I had a most prolific, zealous and relatively accurate historian in John Foxe. Though it may no longer be fashionable to attribute as much significance to Foxe's *Acts and Monuments* – more commonly known as the *Book of Martyrs* and first published in 1563 – as one used to do, Foxe's detailed account of nearly all the executions still evokes strong images and heightened emotions. It cannot be insignificant that the work enjoyed at least five editions in its first quarter-century, and that it came to be one of the most frequently printed works in the English language.

The Protestants in exile

The role of those who stayed at home and endured or suffered under Mary's rule was only slightly more important for the future of English Protestantism than that of the Marian exiles. Beginning in January, 1554, approximately eight hundred English men and women took leave of Mary's Catholic regime and gravitated abroad of their own volition, though some – as they (and Foxe) took pains to establish – were virtually driven abroad by the new regime. Most of them went during the early months of 1554, and some of them returned and then went back again. These Marian exiles did not, for the most part, think of their stay as permanent and the majority made little attempt to blend into the native population of the places where they settled. By and large, they found havens in the freer Protestant cities of the Continent (including Arrau, Basle, Emden, Frankfurt, Geneva, Strasburg, Wesel and Zurich), a few early Huguenot strongholds in France (Rouen and Caen), or in Italy (especially Padua). Like refugee groups at most times they tended to form their own communities, and were successful both in evading much in the way of control from their host communities and in perpetuating their own language and customs.

The composition of the exiles has been analysed as follows: 472 men, 100 wives, 25 women on their own, about 146 children and adolescents and 45 servants, making a total of about 788 (**23**). Those few exiles discovered since this analysis fall roughly into the same proportions. Socially, the largest group of exiles were of gentle birth and there were even a few peers, including Francis, second Earl of Bedford and Katherine, Duchess of Suffolk. The remainder, in order of numbers, were theology students or other intellectuals, clergy, servants, merchants and artisans. The absence of labourers or husbandmen, who made up the bulk of the martyrs in England, must be explained by their lack of resources to travel abroad rather than by any lack of zeal on their part.

Several attempts have been made to evaluate the significance of the exiles to England itself. Christina Garrett saw the whole movement as a planned and orderly exodus, a conspiracy supported politically and financially by sympathisers in England primarily for the purpose of educating a Protestant leadership which might bring true reformation to England on a sunnier day. She noted that during their sojourn abroad the exiles absorbed a great deal of contemporary Protestant thought, much of it Calvinist, and that they worked consciously and constantly toward fomenting a Protestant rising against the Marian regime in England (**23**). Yet, though there was obviously frequent communication between the exiles and their friends or families in England, and though there was undeniably some collaboration for the purpose of smuggling Protestant writings into the realm, the 'conspiracy theory' on the whole has not been sustained by recent research.

A second attempt to explain the significance of the Marian exile experience came in the monumental work of the late Sir John Neale on the parliaments of Elizabeth. Neale thought of the exiles as returning to England at Elizabeth's accession with the conscious intent of forming a powerful interest group in parliament, and of working in that forum to secure a Genevan style reformed Church under Elizabeth (**45**, vol. I). Yet recent research has tended to deny the co-ordinated operation of such a group in Elizabeth's first parliaments, and thus calls into question the presumed extent of organisation or common intent among the returned exiles (**32**).

In explaining the role of the exiles in the development of the Elizabethan church and society there are several points to be considered. Along with the sojourn in England of continental Protestants in Edward's reign, the Marian exile experience provided one of two occasions upon which English men and women enjoyed prolonged and direct contact with the second generation of continental reformers – the generation dominated not by Luther but by Calvin. Though it may not have been expressed quite as Neale saw it, the sum of those experiences contributed greatly to the fundamentally Calvinist tone of mainstream Anglican theology and practice as worked out in the Elizabethan era. In a similar manner, this contact imparted first-hand experience of numerous forms of ecclesiastical organisation which did not necessarily entail the operation of royal supremacy. In their various communities abroad the Marian exiles worked out the essence of the Congregationalist and Presbyterian systems, such as were to make their appearance both in England and in New England in the following century. Finally, their experience provided the opportunity to construct Protestant theories of political opposition which were applicable to English conditions, and these rapidly became incorporated into the controversies both of the Elizabethan and Jacobean eras. In short, the Marian exiles – their horizons broadened by contact with continental ideas, the experience of political and ecclesiastical self-government, and a view of their native land which could only be acquired from abroad – stimulated debates and proposed theories which proved vital to the Elizabethan Settlement and to the Elizabethan state.

Summary

Though it is often forgotten, perhaps the most important reason why Catholicism was never successfully re-implanted in Mary's reign is that that reign itself lasted only a little over five years. Had Mary enjoyed the longevity of her half-sister, who reigned for forty-five, England might well have remained an integral part of the See of Rome.

Yet this accident of life-span should not blind us to some very serious problems regarding the manner in which Mary proceeded. For one thing, the efforts toward Catholic restoration were almost never directed by anyone – with the possible exception of Gardiner – who made an accurate reading of contemporary English religious sentiment. Mary herself had never been out of the realm, but neither had she ever really been in touch with it. Philip could not be expected to recognise the sentiments of a population of which he had virtually no first-hand experience. Pole was the most successful of the three, and must be given this due for accomplishments which have been too little recognised. But even he took England to be as he remembered it rather than as it was and, perhaps burned out from his exhausting battles in the world of papal government, he remained curiously aloof from the more progressive aspects of continental Catholicism with which he had earlier been associated. In consequence, the version of Catholicism which the Marian regime attempted to reintroduce held little to capture the imagination of most Englishmen not already committed to it: no missionary zeal, no particularly positive statements, no influx of money with which to create a 'beauty of holiness', and – save for that 'Mechanik Preacher' of the sixteenth century, Miles Huggarde – not much compelling literary expression.

Perhaps more seriously, the Marian Church appeared not to capitalise on the strength of native English spiritual or intellectual traditions, but rather inclined towards the more repressive attitude represented in the contemporary counter-Reformation by Popes Leo X and Paul IV: a note which struck too few responsive chords in its distinctly English audience. In the end the most significant contribution of the abortive Marian reaction to the formation of a post-Reformation English identity was the exile experience on the one hand and the legacy of persecution – rightly or wrongly connected in the popular mind with the 'Spanish treachery' – on the other.

6 For and Against the Regime: The Battle of Words

Introduction

Conditioned as we are to the realities of political life in the late twentieth century, we tend to expect a conscious and forthright attempt on the part of controversial regimes such as Mary's to engage in what we term public relations. This has become commonplace to us, and was remarkably successful even in the reign of Mary's father. As Geoffrey Elton and others have shown, the government of Henry VIII clearly understood the value of such efforts in justifying the 'new monarchy' of which it was a part. It went to great lengths in the use of tracts, proclamations and sermons, and in creating the variegated splendour of the court itself. The results of this were broadly evident and considerably effective. The citizens of London and, less frequently, other parts of the realm, lined the streets to watch the King pass by and inhaled the aroma of Renaissance monarchy. For their part, the intellectuals of the day, both at home and abroad, could read and consider an impressive array of writings on behalf of the regime, produced by Cranmer, Morison, Latimer and others who worked under the aegis of Thomas Cromwell. These efforts, extending well into the reign of Edward and picked up again by a younger generation under Elizabeth, argued the case for Henrician supremacy and put forward theories of obedience built on reasons of state rather than on theological foundations. They may be credited with turning a majority of the population towards genuine support of the regime and with defining the nature of that regime itself.

Though faced with tasks of similar magnitude, the achievement of Mary's government stands in stark contrast to that of the Henricians. The Queen herself displayed relatively little consciousness of public relations. She neither projected nor attracted the glitter of Renaissance monarchy; she commissioned little in the way of royal portraiture and enticed few poets to praise her virtues; she lacked the Henrician sense of public occasion which would be perfected as a royal art form under Elizabeth.

Lacking inspiration from the throne, and generally incapable of such initiative on its own, Mary's regime concentrated on the suppression of opposing voices rather than the projection of its own. Mary's policy of censorship, which was by no means unique to her reign, was first unveiled in two of her earliest proclamations. These forbade the printing of seditious rumours (28 July 1553) and the 'playing of interludes and printing of false fond books, ballads, rhymes and other lewd treatises . . . concerning doctrine in matters now in question' (18 August 1553). After these opening salvoes the government made further proclamations which had the effect of reviving the Henrician heresy statutes. These included an 'index' of proscribed writers (13 June 1555) and eventually went so far as to proclaim the death penalty even for possession of treasonable books (6 June 1558). In addition, several acts of parliament were passed to make slander against the Queen or King punishable as treason (1 and 2 Ph. & M. c. 3, c. 9 and c. 10). Finally, three different commissions were created by letters patent in 1555 and 1558 'to enquire concerning all heresies, heretical and seditious books, with power to seize all books and writings and to enquire into all enormities' (**80**).

This catalogue of prohibitions may seem rather an elaborate framework for the suppression of heretical or seditious views, but the problem was not as simple as it appears. The attempt to forestall the publication of opposition views within the realm proved inadequate. Many, perhaps even most, of those who wished to write against the regime had gone abroad. In Strasburg, Frankfurt, Geneva, Zurich, Padua and elsewhere they enjoyed the stimulation of travel, new perspectives on their native land, and a fertile philosophical, theological and political milieu in which to work. More practically, they found it easy to publish in virtually any of the cities in which they took shelter and in most instances they were not effectively prevented from smuggling their tracts back across the Channel to their intended audiences.

Furthermore, when Protestantism did not melt away as Mary had hoped, it became important to consider the continued availability of Protestant service books, especially the Prayer Book of 1552, upon which the perpetuation of that faith depended. The most recent historian of the Tudor printing trade has estimated that close to 19,000 copies of this crucial work must have existed in the realm at Mary's accession – enough to sustain a viable Protestant underground for some time to come (**101**). In addition, even the government's efforts at suppression were not carried out with much consistency. While there were numerous prosecutions of 'seditious writers', and while there were earnest efforts to prevent the smuggling of books, there was little effective attempt to silence such imprisoned Protestant leaders as Latimer and Ridley, whose pamphlets and letters continued to pour forth unimpeded from their Oxford jail. A telling measure of this failure is the conclusion that the most original, stimulating and even the most numerous writings of the reign were produced by the Protestants (**78**).

Voices in opposition

Though a large proportion of the work of the Marian exiles does survive, and though they wrote and published in virtually all the cities which sheltered them for any significant time, it is impossible to be precise regarding the volume of their literary production. Some of their writings failed to reach their intended audience; some have not survived for posterity; a number were never actually set in type and run off. Nonetheless, it seems reasonable to suggest that the volume of Protestant writings was some twenty per cent greater than that of Catholic efforts, with most, though not all, of them being published abroad (**7, 105**).

In the Protestant literature which survives from Mary's reign, several categories may be distinguished. A large number of those publications which dealt with religious questions (and not all of them did) were fairly traditional statements, often counselling outward submission to official doctrines. These tended to explain that God had visited Mary's regime upon the faithful as punishment for their sins, and that the duty of the good Christian was one of obedience and endurance for as long as necessary: e.g., Thomas Becon, *A Comfortable Epistle too Goddes faythfull People in Englande* . . .; John Scory, *An epistle written unto all the faythfull that be in pryson in Englande* (**78**).

Others urged passive disobedience, counselling their readers to refuse to attend mass, encouraging the perpetuation of Protestant rites and generally attempting to infuse courage into the hearts of all opponents of Mary's religious policies: e.g., Anon., *Whether Christian Faith maye be kepte secret in the heart* (probably an English translation of a work by Calvin himself).

Some opposition writers dealt with specific political issues, in which religious concerns took a back seat to what may only be defined as an early English patriotism. Most of these tracts were prompted by specific events in England, demonstrating yet again the ability of the exiles to keep closely in touch with news from home. Often, in fact, opposition writers in exile were quicker to capitalise on such occasional opportunities than Mary's own supporters. The Spanish match, and the foreign influence which was expected to come with it, proved obvious targets, as was shown by the anonymous *Warnyng for Englande, conteyning the horrible practises of the King of Spayne, in the Kingdom of Naples*. The threat that former church lands would be confiscated from their present owners, emphasised in John Knox's *A faythfull admonition*, must have cut close to the bone for many of its readers, and remained a major concern in Mary's parliaments up to and even after Pole's concession on this point (**78**).

The tactic of reprinting works of continental writers, usually in English translation, was another common device of the exile press. Not only were the works of such Protestant worthies as Luther, Melanchthon, and Calvin made available to an English audience, but also some writings by Catholics – like the papal bull of 1555 against the alienation of Church lands – which were calculated to embarrass the government or cast doubt upon its policies.

These, then, were the central aims of the expatriates' writings: to undermine the credibility of the Marian regime, to sustain the hopes and faith of English Protestants at home, to move the more literate and courageous toward passive disobedience and, especially in the last months of the reign, to hurl invective at Mary and her government.

Though they were largely unrepresentative of this majority, a few writers went further, and by 1556 were developing, for perhaps the first time among English Protestants, theories of active disobedience. The best known of this small band were John Knox and his close associate Christopher Goodman, who worked first in Frankfurt and then moved on to Geneva; and John Ponet, who fled abroad early in 1554 and spent the rest of his time in Strasburg, where he died in 1556.

Goodman, born in England, and Knox, born in Scotland, worked closely together during most of their stay abroad, and were closely identified with each other in that intense debate over the nature of the Church known as the 'troubles at Frankfurt'. Although both must be considered among the more radical Calvinists in England during the hegemony of Northumberland, neither had experienced any occasion to develop opposition theories. Exile provided that impetus, and even then it took a few years for them to move away from Calvin's emphasis on the need for obedience. Although they did ultimately break with Calvin and his more orthodox followers on this crucial issue, they still kept ever before them the goal of establishing a 'Calvinist' society. Indeed, they helped organise such a community for their fellow exiles in Geneva, and must therefore still be counted as a part of that doctrinal school.

Of the two, Knox probably provoked a more intense contemporary reaction but possibly had less impact over the long term on English (as opposed to Scottish) thought. This was not merely because he took as his chief theme the illegitimacy of women rulers as measured by natural law. The long reign of Elizabeth, and her willingness to incorporate at least some of the tenets of Calvinist practice, rendered Knox anathema to many, and an uncomfortable companion to others. In Scotland, his views were easily triumphant in the successful effort to overthrow a 'tyrannical' woman and establish a Calvinist regime. In *The First Blast of the Trumpet Against the Monstrous Regiment of Women* of 1558, however, Knox took what he saw as the calamities which had befallen England – particularly her subordination to Spanish influence and to a foreign and idolatrous religion – as proof of God's displeasure at the unnatural choice of Mary as Queen. In *The Appellation of John Knox* of 1558 he argued even more forcefully that women rulers must be overthrown.

Christopher Goodman served with laudable success as the elected minister of the English exile community in Geneva. Under his direction that community not only flourished as a model of harmony and Christian purpose, but produced two works which came in Elizabeth's reign to play vital roles in the formation of English Protestantism: the Geneva Bible and the quasi-constitutional handbook entitled *The Forme of Prayers and ministration of the Sacraments*. Goodman himself felt obliged by 1556 to go beyond the usual Protestant views on obedience and the nature of monarchy. His sermon-turned-essay *How Superior Powers ought to be Obeyed* (1556) was not only one of the few statements of the doctrine of resistance to come out of the exile experience, but was also one of the most politically practical of such statements in the literature of sixteenth-century political thought. What made it so was both the clarity with which Goodman specified particular courses of action, and the manner in which he combined a fundamentally theological attack on Mary with a more broadly secular call to the colours directed toward his fellow Englishmen.

Goodman put forward a concept of limited monarchy in which the monarch held his or her authority from God, but only at the election of the people. Such election took the form of a covenant. The King remained obliged, as 'one of the brethren', to show fear of God and respect for His word, and not to rule by coercion. He was also accountable to the people for the discharge of his godly obligations. For their part, the people were bound to remain obedient to a godly monarch, but were equally bound to enforce God's will against an ungodly ruler. This they were not merely entitled to do if they chose, but were obliged to do as God's people, even to the point of disobedience or actual revolution. Thus Mary, having clearly belied God's trust according to Goodman's criteria, had now to be deposed by the magistrates of the realm – the nobles, councillors and justices – acting on behalf of the people at large. Should the magistrates themselves fail in that responsibility, the people were obliged to undertake it themselves (**95**).

Though Goodman's ideas seemed warranted to some Englishmen at the time, they proved embarrassingly extreme after the return of Protestantism under Elizabeth. Goodman himself felt compelled to spend his remaining days across the Scottish border, and his political thought remained largely unacknowledged for the remainder of the century. In the trying times of the following century, however, Goodman's ideas again found an attentive audience, and inspired John Milton and others of that era.

Superficially, John Ponet's ideas seem somewhat similar to Goodman's, though not to Knox's. Yet Ponet, writing in Strasburg rather than Geneva, worked independently of the others, and his views smack much less of the Calvinist tradition. In his *Short Treatise of Politike Power*, published in 1556, Ponet also argued against the absolutist nature of royal authority, emphasising the ruler's obligation to protect the common weal of which he, like the people, was a part. Yet although Ponet wrote vividly of the right of the people to depose an unjust monarch, he never described, as Goodman had done, the specific means whereby Mary ought to be brought to justice (**30**).

Marian voices

By comparison with these numerous, often vibrant and sometimes quite original writings of the English Protestants in exile, the polemical output of the Marians was slight in both quality and quantity. Of the non-literary varieties of government propaganda which Mary's government seems to have employed, only the proclamations fulfilled much more than the role of public relations.

The practice of sponsoring Sunday sermons at Paul's Cross in London, which previous regimes had employed to bring quasi-official messages to the populace from the most prestigious pulpit in the land, was by no means forgotten under Mary. Yet following the public reaction to the first such sermon in the reign – in which Gilbert Bourne was nearly struck by a dagger thrown from the crowd after advocating the release from prison of the Catholic Edmund Bonner – the government seems to have employed this device less frequently and to have it treated it with less importance than its predecessors had done. Among the chief spokesmen for the Marian regime, Nicholas Harpsfield, archdeacon of Canterbury, used the occasion twice: once (dutifully and courageously, for the event was most unpopular) to praise the marriage of Philip to Mary, and once to give thanks for victory over the French at St Quentin. Gardiner used that forum to praise Philip in September, 1554, and again, in perhaps the most striking Paul's Cross sermon of the reign, to announce the reconciliation with Rome in early December, 1554. But beyond this the sermons were delivered less frequently and by lesser men than either before or after Mary's reign. Thus the government made relatively scant use of an import-ant platform for the propagation of its views (**42**).

The regime's record in written polemic is scarcely more impress-ive. Of the pro-government writers the most remarkable was the obscure Miles Huggard (or Hogard), a London hosier with no known academic or ecclesiastical background. Huggard was hardly an official spokesman, as his only government appointment seems to have been as the Queen's Hosier, but he was eloquent, prolific, and even original in defence of the Marian regime and the old faith. Ironically, the Protestant opposition took him more seriously than did the government, for although his chief tract, *The Displaying of the Protestants* of 1556, drew rebuffs from some half dozen of the Protestants whom he attacked in it, he remained ever an outsider at court, an appealing and mysterious 'mechanik preacher' of the Catholic cause (**104**). Along with Huggard, John Gwynneth, John Standish, and the Queen's chaplain, John Christopherson, were most prolific in the Queen's defence, but their names – save per-haps for the last – remain justly obscure in any discussion of Tudor ideas.

As far as themes are concerned, a large number of the Marian writings seem to have been inspired by Reginald Pole's clerically based strategy for restoring the Catholic faith and were directed toward counselling the priesthood in its duties. John Angel's *The agrement of the holye fathers* (1555), Richard Smith's *A Bouclier of the Catholike Faythe* (1554), and Bishop Bonner's 'Book of Homilies' (*A Profitable and necessarye doctryne*) of 1555 – largely written by his archdeacon, John Harpsfield – are prime examples of this vein (**94**).

A closely related theme was the exposition of the Church's views on doctrinal matters – as in Thomas Watson's *Twoo Notable Sermons ... Concernyng the Real Presence* (1554) and his *Holsome and Catholyke doctryne concernying the seuon sacramentes* (1558). Another common theme, though hardly more original than the first two, was the exhortation to obedience. James Cancellar's *The Pathe of Obedience* (1553), and Christopherson's *Exhortation to all menne to take hede of rebellion* . . . (1554) are standard fare in this respect. The latter takes as its point of departure Wyatt's Rising, yet it is an interesting commentary on the government's responsiveness that it appeared well after both the event itself and the commentary upon it written by several Protestants.

A final category of Marian writing consists of a small body of works intended specifically to discredit the spokesmen of Protestantism or its practice in previous reigns. Northumberland's *Saying uppon the Scaffolde* (1553), Cranmer's *Submyssyons and Recantations* (1556) and even John Proctor's *Historie of Wyates Rebellion* (1554) all fit this mould. Yet even here the regime was less than efficient in pursuing its potential advantage. It missed a priceless opportunity for propaganda when the eminent Protestant humanist John Cheke was kidnapped abroad, brought back to England, and made to confess his transgressions against the government before the Queen and members of the Privy Chamber. Though this episode struck deeply at the morale of the remaining exiles, who learned of it rapidly enough through their excellent grapevine, it is astounding that no one at court thought of publishing the submission for distribution in England (**7**).

How can we account for the limited quantity and mundane quality of the pro-Marian writings? It is no doubt appropriate to suggest that Mary herself failed to inspire the intellectuals of her day as her father or Thomas Cromwell had done, but that observation begs a number of questions in turn. For one, Mary's government neither recruited nor otherwise attracted the sort of articulate and resourceful men who were welcomed to the court in the 1530s, many of them straight from such humanist centres as Padua and most of them steeped in the heady brew of continental ideas. Few of Mary's advisers, and especially not the Catholic backwoodsmen with whom she felt most comfortable, had studied abroad as had Starkey, Morison, Armstrong or their fellows; few of them shared the broadened intellect or traditions of polemical debate cultivated by such experience. Beyond that, most of the bright lights of the 1530s and 40s were Protestants, and indeed it is difficult to separate the liberal and humanist ideas of such men as Morison, Smith, Latimer and Ridley from their distinctly Protestant outlook.

Yet this facility for lively, progressive and highly polemical thought and writing had not always been a Protestant preserve. The vast majority of early 'Christian humanists' in England as on the continent – men like Erasmus, More, and their contemporaries – may have inspired the thinkers of the 1530s and 40s, but nearly all of them had pointedly and even courageously rejected the Protestantism made acceptable by that younger generation. Since their time, however, that Erasmian vitality had withered within the universal Catholic Church: such leaders as Erasmus and the Italian Gaspar Contarini had died, leaving no intellectual heirs of equal capacity behind them, while the brilliant Bernardino Ochino had stunned reform-minded Catholics throughout Europe by defecting to Protestantism in 1542. Reformist hopes were further dashed by the reactionary tide which set in at the Council of Trent (1545–1563) not long after it opened.

Thus, by the time of Mary's accession in 1553, those Englishmen who might have exemplified Erasmian humanism, political openness, or even straightforward polemical ability had no wellspring upon which to draw within the continental Catholicism of the day. While a few works of More and Erasmus were reprinted under Mary (as they were under the Protestant Elizabeth, for that matter) such former spokesmen for reformed Catholicism as Pole himself and his fellow Catholic countrymen who had been nurtured under his wing at Padua – George Lily, Henry Cole, and even the privy councillor John Mason – remained too aloof, too preoccupied (like Pole himself), or simply too dispirited to provide inspiration for the defence of the regime. In consequence, those who did wield their pens on behalf of the Marian cause were generally lightweights, utterly outclassed by the sly, seasoned and crafty heavyweights of English Protestantism in exile.

As if this was not enough, there was also a practical problem with the composition and publication of pro-government views which the regime's opponents abroad did not experience to the same extent. Too few publishers remained in England after 1553 or early 1554, and they had to produce too many 'service' books of one sort or another to leave much time or inclination for more expository work. The number of foreign and Protestant printers who left the realm or stopped publishing after Mary's accession was both large and uncompensated for by the addition of new recruits to the trade. There may well have been only half as many printers at work in Mary's reign as before, yet they were called on to produce in vast quantities the entire range of printed material essential for the restoration of Catholic worship throughout the realm. It was very much the concern of Pole and his bishops – and rightly so – that the clergy should have at their disposal sufficient missals, hymnals, homilies, breviaries, primers, psalters, and other tools of their trade to perform their key role. But the provision of this material did not simply take up a great deal of time and energy; it also ensured a ready and profitable market for the printers and made them less willing to produce and sell polemical works with limited readership (**101**).

For all these reasons – the government's own lack of inspiration, the limited ability of many of the people whom it attracted to its service, the unresolved tensions within the Catholic Church as a whole, the down-to-earth outlook of leaders like Pole, and the conditions prevailing within the publishing industry at that time – the polemical output of Mary's reign was not impressive in quality or quantity. The works of its opponents, on the other hand, which were often more readily printed and easily enough smuggled into the realm, were just as often more significant in content and more inspired in tone. It is thus ironic but plausible to see the link between the so-called Commonwealth men prior to 1553, and such Elizabethan humanist writers as Sir Thomas Smith and Bishop John Jewel, not in the Marian regime itself, but rather in the Protestant opposition in exile.

7 Economic and Social Issues

Introduction

As indicated earlier, in the background section of this book, Mary's reign came in the midst of several long-term, profound, and painfully unsettling transitions in social and economic activity. It was then suggested that the roots of those problems were sufficiently deep to preclude the assignment of responsibility for them to any single government, and certainly not to Mary's. It remains in this chapter to discuss in somewhat more concrete terms how the Marian regime attempted to deal with some of those difficulties, to evaluate its success, and to place its efforts in the wider context of Tudor domestic policy and administration.

The most important areas of Marian activity included (1) the regime's efforts to facilitate better commercial relations abroad; (2) its attempts to strengthen the government's fiscal resources, largely through reform of the customs system; (3) its forthright intervention, often for the first time, in domestic commerce and industry; (4) its responsive interest in the problems of towns and cities; and (5) the resourceful initiatives which it took toward problems of charity and welfare.

Commercial relations

Following Mary's accession, relations between the crown and the overseas merchants of the realm took some time to stabilise. For several years prior to 1553 English sales both of wool, monopolised by the Merchants of the Staple at Calais on the Norman coast, and of woollen cloth, monopolised among English traders by the Merchant Adventurers, had begun to falter. Edward's government reacted to this by placing a ban on the purchase of English cloth in England by the merchants of the Hanseatic League (1552). In addition, it had reconsidered the Henrician policy of sponsoring exploratory sea voyages in the hope of finding new markets; the navigator Thomas Wyndham, for example, was despatched in 1551 and again in 1553 to the coast of Africa. Yet these were tentative initiatives, and Mary's regime met them with uncertainty.

Shortly after her accession, in an effort to secure better ties with the important trading powers of the Baltic coast, Mary lifted the ban on Hanseatic purchases of cloth in England, thus earning the anger of her own Merchant Adventurers. However, in 1555 she began a shift in policy, completed two years later, which led to the reimposition of the ban (**58**, pp. 226–7). By then, in the words of one economic historian, 'The Merchant Adventurers [had] more than recovered the position they seem to have lost with the accession of Mary Tudor' (**52**, p. 69).

The Merchants of the Staple fared less well. For a variety of reasons, mostly having to do with the nature of international markets in the early sixteenth century and the rising price of raw wool in England, the Staple at Calais had languished for some years prior to 1553. So feeble had that last English enclave on the continent become that by 1540 the merchant community fell to some 150 traders, and the community became dependent on food imports to sustain itself. By the middle of Mary's reign attempts were under way to find a suitable alternative to Calais as a home for the Staplers, and both before and after the actual fall of Calais itself to the French in 1557, Bergen, Bruges and Middleburg were all tried on an experimental basis. In the end, the problem remained unsolved, and the sale of raw English wool abroad simply ceased to be a viable trading venture. In large measure this may be explained by the increased competition between the wool merchants who made their living from exporting, and those who bought wool in order to supply cloth manufacturers at home. That competition simply drove up the Staplers' costs to the point where the wool of other nations, especially Spain, became much more competitive on the international market.

In order to compensate for this weakness in one aspect of English foreign trade, and no doubt with an eye to public opinion as well, Mary had hoped to gain some commercial advantages through her ties with Spain. As part of her marriage treaty with Philip, English merchants were supposed to enjoy limited access for the first time to the riches of South America. Unfortunately, this expectation was never fulfilled. While the Atlantic trade routes remained effectively closed to Englishmen Mary was too closely linked with Spanish interests to permit the sort of freelance encroachment on Spanish preserves which the Elizabethans would undertake with zeal. Thus, while the government became convinced more than ever of the

Analysis

necessity of new trade routes, the Spanish alliance effectively guaranteed nothing more than continued ties with the valuable Dutch markets. Though this was far from insignificant, it was not sufficient.

With the need for new markets clearly in view, Mary's government saw the potential of late Edwardian inclinations to move eastward toward Russia and the Baltic, and it pressed as well for an important commercial foothold in Africa. In the first instance Marian government encouraged the commercial expansion into Russia which was to be so strategically important in the days of naval warfare under Elizabeth. The first contacts were established through the exploratory voyages of Stephen Borough and Anthony Jenkinson in Mary's reign, following in the wake of the Edwardian explorers Sir Hugh Willoughby (who froze to death off Lapland a few months after Mary's accession) and Richard Chancellor. Formal links were signified by the chartering of the Muscovy Company in 1555, which imported valuable naval supplies and sold the Russians herbs, woollens and metalwork in return (**51, 60**).

Marian initiatives in the Baltic matured more slowly. Their fulfilment came only when war closed Antwerp to English shipping in the 1560s, and the Eastland Company – the Baltic counterpart to the Muscovy Company – was not founded until 1579. Yet here again Marian initiatives lay at the root of the later achievement.

In the opposite direction, meanwhile, Marian traders established, with government encouragement, small but important footholds in Morocco and Guinea. Based largely on the voyages of Thomas Wyndham in Edward's reign and John Lok and William Towerson in Mary's, both provided an outlet for the 'new draperies' which were beginning to come out of England, while providing in return sugar and saltpetre from Morocco and gold from Guinea (**58**).

These efforts of the crown and council on behalf of English traders may not always have been entirely successful, especially in the case of the Merchant Staplers. Yet they mark an important step in the emerging alliance between the Tudor monarchy and the commercial interests of its subjects. Not only does this new alliance stand in contrast to the Henrician policy of non-involvement, but it may also be seen as a counterweight to the presumed – and largely overstated – commercial decline which followed the loss of Calais. A telling attestation to the good relations which developed between the crown and the merchant community in Mary's reign was the almost complete lack of protest from traders against the higher Customs duties imposed by the new Book of Rates in 1558.

Customs

One of the most serious and least understood problems of the Tudor monarchy was its difficulty in financing the costs of government. This difficulty arose because of a growing discrepancy between the increasing expenses of post-medieval government and the limited yield of a still fundamentally medieval fiscal structure. The costs of government grew for many reasons, not the least of which were the unremitting surge of inflation, the escalating scale of sixteenth-century warfare, the larger scope of government activity, and the higher expenditures entailed by the Tudors' 'Renaissance style' of kingship.

Tudor regimes attempted to cope with this constant predicament in several ways, though only Henry VII, who managed to avoid warfare, left a solvent crown. Apart from the sale of crown lands, offices and monopolies, most of the Tudors relied to a preponderant extent on parliamentary subsidies: a means of raising revenue which before the sixteenth century had been considered appropriate only in 'extraordinary' circumstances. Though subsidies brought in ready cash in a relatively short time, they entailed distinct political risk, and could not be demanded too often. Although Mary certainly requested subsidies, as her predecessors had done, she relied more than any other Tudor monarch on expanding sources of 'ordinary' revenue, most of which could be collected by prerogative right rather than by consent of parliament. Chief among such sources was the customs.

The yield of the customs depended on the rates of assessment, the efficiency of collection, and of course on the volume of trade. Having taken steps to increase trade, Mary's regime now sought to ensure at least a proportionate increase in customs receipts. Well might it have done so, for in addition to increasing costs of government (especially those brought on by the war begun in 1557) the existing duties were hopelessly outmoded. Based on standard rates promulgated in 1507 and only slightly revised in 1536 and 1545, the system left entirely untaxed literally hundreds of commodities. In addition, duties were anachronistically based on an export trade in which raw wool figured more prominently than woollen cloth, and they depended on valuations which had been rendered altogether obsolete by the inflation rate of approximately 350 per cent between 1507 and 1558 (**47**, fig. I, p. 11).

Mary's predecessors had not been blind to the need to revise customs duties. Northumberland's advisers had urged him to adopt a new Book of Rates in 1552, and this recommendation proved the genesis of the Marian revision promulgated in 1558. This revised schedule increased the number of valuations on imports alone from about 790 to 1,170 and placed most of the burden on non-essential goods in the hope of fostering native industry at a time of high unemployment (**18, 59**).

Perhaps the most influential aspect of the new Book, however, was the actual extent of revaluation in which duties were brought into line with current values. In all, the average increase in valuation over the 1545 revision has been estimated at an astonishing 118.8 per cent (**59**, pp. xxiii–xxiv)! In retrospect, it is nothing less than remarkable that, despite her severe financial problems and apparent difficulties with some of her parliaments, Elizabeth made only two revisions in the Marian customs rates, neither of them of much consequence. The Marian Book of Rates survived substantially unamended until 1604 (**59**) [**doc. 9**].

As for the efficiency of collection, the very structure of the customs system which Mary inherited was virtually guaranteed to bring a yield which, even by Tudor standards, was substantially below potential. This became a second objective in Mary's reforms. In imitation of the system for the administration of crown lands, the office of Surveyor General of the Customs was created and granted (at least for the port of London) to Sir Francis Englefield. The concept seems to have come from William Paulet, Marquis of Winchester, probably the most astute of all the Marian councillors in economic and fiscal affairs. Winchester had hoped to extend the Surveyor's jurisdiction to the whole realm, and saw that step accomplished for the first time under Elizabeth. Yet in the end his judicious preference for a centralised control of customs gave rise by the 1570s to the more politically expedient idea of 'farming it out' to professional collectors working on a commission basis. Thus was a promising Marian initiative reversed in Elizabeth's reign (**18**).

Finally, the Marian regime seems to have been responsible for the introduction of impositions, those bugbears of early Stuart parliaments, as an additional expedient for raising revenues from trade. Mary's levy of August, 1554 on sweet wines was the first application of this prerogative power, and at least three other such instances followed in the course of the reign. Although the practice was not challenged by Mary's parliaments, it was appealed against in the Court of the Exchequer in 1559, thus beginning a lengthy and interesting chapter in the history of the royal prerogative.

Domestic commerce and industry

The theme of increased government involvement which runs through these elements of English commercial activity may also be recognised in the domestic scene. Just as it had worked closely with merchants trading abroad and sought to benefit directly from any growth in their enterprises, so did the Marian regime become more closely involved with such institutions as gilds and other traditional economic interests, with towns and boroughs, and with those who sought to generate an institutionalised charitable response to the poverty and disease so rampant in that era.

The first of these subjects – that of the gilds and other traditional economic interests – is the most sparingly treated in existing literature, but the evidence for it seems clear enough. Faced with the changing patterns of trade and industry which have been outlined above, Tudor governments had essentially three courses of action open to them. They could have continued to do little, as had been the 'policy by default' before the 1540s. They might have tried to reinforce the familiar patterns of the traditional, pre-capitalistic economy, by such measures as strengthening the gilds, enforcing the apprenticeship laws and restricting the mobility of workers and craftsmen. Or, finally, they could have leapt into the dark and supported what we now recognise as the forces of early capitalist free enterprise: permitting or even encouraging the growth of rural industry, facilitating the flow of credit and capital, and approving of the migration of labour.

The single best known response to that dilemma is the famous Statute of Artificers of 1563, in which the Elizabethan government effectively adopted the middle choice, trying to roll back the tide of change, and to reinforce the old restrictions on conditions of manufacture, sale, and employment. Given the state of economic and social analysis of that time, late Tudor governments may perhaps be exonerated from much of the blame which our hindsight leads us to attach to that choice. Fortification of the familiar against the tides of change was perhaps the most reasonable course which lay open to them. But any credit for choosing this course should not be given to Elizabeth's government alone, nor should it be assumed that the 1563 statute initiated such a policy. This course was well under way in Mary's reign, and may have been foreshadowed even in Edward's.

At the same time that it broke decisively with the policy of non-involvement in foreign trade, Mary's regime appears also to have lent greater support to traditional institutions in the domestic economy than its predecessors had done. Following the Woollen Cloth Act of Edward's reign (5 Edw. VI c. 6), three separate acts of Mary's reign pointed in the direction which the 1563 statute was to follow. The Retail Trades Act of 1554 (1 and 2 Ph. & M. c. 7) protected the retail monopoly of merchants operating within corporate limits from unregulated competition. The Weavers' Act of 1552 (2 and 3 Ph. & M. c. 11) made it more difficult to weave cloth outside existing corporate regulations of towns or gilds. The Woollen Cloth Act of 1557 (4 and 5 Ph. & M. c. 5) was the most sweeping legislation of the century on the manufacture of England's chief industrial product, and similarly placed heavy fines on manufacturers of cloth outside traditional jurisdictions.

Town and crown

In a closely related vein, Mary's government received a very great number of pleas and plaints from impoverished towns, where the responsibility of relieving the poor and sick compounded the stresses imposed by broader economic changes. Although the Marian regime was not the first to receive such complaints in large number, it was clearly experiencing the post-Reformation tendency of towns, now devoid of most of the institutions which had been run by the pre-Reformation Church, to look more to Westminster for support and relief. In response, Mary's government offered what help it could, and sometimes profited by the knowledge of local initiatives which it gained in the process. Thus more than one 'national policy', including poor relief and the provision of public grain stocks, was first implemented by specific town governments. The goals of this relatively perceptive urban outlook of the Marian regime included both urban recovery and the attainment of social stability in the centres of population by assuring strong, loyal governments at that level.

An increasingly common form of response to urban complaints in this period was the grant of a charter of incorporation. Typically, these were issued after considerable negotiation in response to petitions from towns themselves, whose leading citizens hoped to reinforce their authority by such a device. Mary's regime granted more than twice as many such charters per year as her predecessors, and in so doing it worked toward a uniform standard for the structure and powers of municipal governments. To the recipient town, incorporation confirmed existing rights or created new ones. It permitted towns to act as corporate entities before the law with perpetual succession of their governments; to hold land 'in mortmain' which could be sold or let – an essential means of obtaining revenue for schools, relief institutions, public works and the like; to use a corporate seal; to issue by-laws; and generally to fend for themselves more effectively in competition with other towns and the surrounding countryside [**doc. 10**]. It is perhaps some measure of the success of these policies that a surprising number of towns still employed their Marian charters of incorporation as their chief instruments of government even up to the eve of the Municipal Corporations Act of 1835 (**92, 91**).

A further theme of government response to the economic and social calamities of the age was that of poor relief and charitable institutions. For a variety of reasons, as discussed above, the Marian years may well have seen a more pressing need for relief of poverty than any comparable period in the century. Mary's government and her parliaments responded to this in a variety of ways. In London, where the problem was perhaps most acute, Mary's council presided over the private initiative of several leading citizens in welding five London charities – St Bartholomew's, St Thomas's, Bethlam, Christ's and the Bridewell – into a city-wide system of social welfare. Active government concern for the plight of the poor was also directed toward the rest of the realm, as Mary employed her power of proclamation, and her council its powers of enforcement, to provide for the distribution of grain wherever it was most required. Indeed, Marian government distinguished itself by its enforcement of laws against grain hoarders, by undertaking systematic surveys of grain stocks in several of the worst hit areas, and by supporting a host of local initiatives toward similar ends. In 1557 it experimented in Yorkshire with the notion of appointing JPs as overseers of the poor, thus trying out what would become an important part of the poor law legislation of Elizabeth's reign. Finally, Mary's parliament of 1555 re-emphasised the importance of converting pasture land to tillage, and the provisions for enforcing this statute were more stringent than anything in the better known anti-enclosure legislation of the previous reigns (**87**).

Mary's government undertook two further initiatives which figured significantly in the development of the English economy. First, it took steps to reform the coinage. Second, it continued efforts to rationalise the structure of central administration.

It was once assumed that the minting of coins came to a virtual halt within two years of Mary's accession, but it is now apparent that minting continued right through Mary's reign, and that the great Elizabethan recoinage of 1560–61 was planned almost in its entirety by Mary's advisers between 1556 and 1558. These plans had to be laid aside in the critical last year of Mary's reign, when the demands of war, pestilence and near famine were all-absorbing, and it was left to Elizabeth's government to put them into effect. Yet, in the words of the historian of the Tudor coinage, 'Elizabeth could never have tackled the problem of the coinage either so quickly or as effectively as she did had it not been so thoroughly aired amongst government officials in the immediately preceding years' (**11**, p. 118).

Mary's efforts to amalgamate the various revenue courts were part of a long-range plan set into motion by Thomas Cromwell more than a decade and a half prior to her accession. Thus the courts of Augmentations and First Fruits and Tenths were duly amalgamated into the Exchequer in the first eighteen months of her reign, according to previous intentions. But in two respects Mary left her own stamp on this process. First, she insisted (against the advice of her Exchequer officials) on the adoption of some of the more advanced methods of auditing and accounting which had been developed in the old King's Chamber (**53**, pp. 109, 433). Second, she decided to preserve the Court of Wards intact rather than proceed with its amalgamation into the Exchequer as planned. This may well have given the Court of Wards a new lease of life, which enabled it to serve throughout Elizabeth's reign as a relatively efficient and lucrative source of revenue (**31, 76**).

Summary

When examined in the context of England's social and economic situation through the middle of the sixteenth century, Mary's regime presents several distinguishing features. The most outstanding of these were the demographic crises which affected at least two-thirds of her short reign, the economically and psychologically costly war which began in 1557, and, on the other side of the ledger, the government's greater involvement in the nation's economy. Yet most economic and social issues were not new in kind after 1553, and the Marians proved no less competent than their predecessors in coping with their adversity.

In 1910 A. F. Pollard pronounced a notorious and enduring verdict on Mary's reign, condemning it as a 'sterile' interlude in Tudor history. It may indeed be the case that the period 1553–58 lacked some of the analytical creativity of the so-called 'Commonwealth men' who served Henry VIII and Edward. Those fascinating individuals, who may or may not have had enough in common to justify the label affixed to them, were simply not at home in the Marian age. Yet this did not prevent Mary's councillors, the governing bodies of her boroughs, or the Queen herself from adopting some of their ideas. At heart these leaders were thorough pragmatists, meeting problems as they came and with whatever solutions seemed attractive at the time.

Given these characteristics of administration, can we detect a clear improvement in the state of the English economy or society during the five and a half years of Marian rule? The short answer would probably be 'not much', but that judgment requires qualification. In line with other governments, the Marians strove to maintain law and order, fiscal stability, and an adequate defence against external threats. As far as law and order are concerned it must be noted that, despite both the appearance of *political* revolt in 1554, and ample cause for *social* unrest, Mary's reign witnesses no violent social or economic risings similar to the Cornish Rising of 1497, the Pilgrimage of Grace of 1536, or both the Western Rising and Ket's Rebellion in 1549. On the second count, Mary clearly did add to the burden of debt, (especially in conducting the war with France) which grew larger with every one of Henry VII's direct descendants. Yet at the same time she seems to have imposed conscious austerity at court and in her household; she made the customs system a potential and inestimably valuable source of crown revenue; she devised a plan to restore the integrity of the coinage; and she saved a lucrative revenue court from amalgamation. Indeed one may only wonder how much more successful Elizabeth's regime might have been if the first two initiatives had been sustained.

In social and economic terms, therefore, Mary's reign marked no sharp break with the past as it did in her religious policy. Continuity, not disruption, was the prevailing theme, but continuity should not be taken to mean complacency. The creative impulse

Analysis

may have changed its form from the earlier humanist impetus, but gave rise nonetheless to a number of innovative policies, some of which bore fruit only after Mary's death. Innovation within a traditional framework of ideas, rather than administrative sterility or collapse, became the hallmark of Mary's regime on social and administrative issues.

8   Myths and Realities in Foreign Affairs

England and Europe in 1553

At the accession of Mary Tudor, European politics were still dominated by the conflict between Valois and Habsburg. This conflict was taking place, as it had for most of the century, on three major fronts: in the territory of the old Burgundian Duchy, roughly conforming to the modern Benelux nations; in Italy; and indirectly in the German states of the Holy Roman Empire where the Protestant princes received some French support in their efforts to gain autonomy from the Emperor Charles. The most recent round of hostilities had brought both sides close to exhaustion, but it had proved especially difficult for the Habsburgs. The French had captured the important city of Metz in 1552, and in the same year the Emperor found himself virtually compelled to concede a degree of autonomy to some of the defiant German princes – a foretaste of the great Peace of Augsburg of 1555.

England, of course, had traditionally been allied with the Habsburgs against the French, and even in the 1540s France remained the 'natural' enemy. Yet under the Duke of Northumberland English policy had undergone a considerable turnabout. He distrusted Charles and the Habsburgs not only as dogged defenders of Roman Catholicism but, even more important, as open supporters of Princess Mary and her Catholic commitment. Yet he also greatly feared – as had Somerset before him – the ability of the French to invade England through the Kingdom of Scotland. The tie between France and Scotland was an old one, but it took on new importance when James V died in 1542, leaving behind his widow, Mary of Guise, and his infant daughter Mary. During Northumberland's period of power, and into Mary Tudor's reign as well, the young Queen of Scotland was being reared at the French court, while Mary of Guise remained in Scotland where she brought French influence to bear in support of the Catholic party. Northumberland's response to such close Franco-Scottish ties, and also to the deteriorating situation in England, was to maintain friendly relations with the French and armed preparedness on the Scottish borders. He also strove to keep the Habsburgs, and especially their dangerous influence on the political attitude of English Catholics, at arm's length.

Mary's accession was an enormous relief to the ageing and weary Emperor Charles V. He looked for a rich return for his long defence of her interests and for the restoration of Anglo-Habsburg amity. The outcome of the ensuing diplomatic battle for Mary's friendship between the French Ambassador de Noailles and the Imperial spokesman Simon Renard was hardly ever in doubt, and the resulting marriage agreement between Mary and Philip gave Charles the confidence and security to go ahead with his plan to abdicate. But what would the treaty bring for England? Would Mary succeed in avoiding entanglement in the Franco-Spanish conflict, as the treaty had promised, or did that ambiguously worded clause refer simply to the phase of that conflict which was taking place in 1554? Would the French resort to harassment through Scotland after all? Would the alliance justify its promise commercially by gaining access for English merchants to the Spanish Atlantic treasure house? These questions remained to be answered.

In the early part of her reign Mary demonstrated an ardent desire to remain at peace and even to act as the mediator between the European powers. From the last months of 1553 through the following year both France and Spain continually intimated, without committing themselves, that Mary might do well to arrange peace negotiations. In the spring of 1555 Mary did finally succeed in bringing both sides to the table, and employed the most impressive talents at her disposal, from Pole downwards, in talks at Gravelines. Yet each side seems to have expected major concessions from the other, and when Spain proved unwilling to return Milan, and France proved equally obdurate regarding Metz and Verdun, the talks stalled. When it was learned in late May that the Neapolitan Cardinal Gian Pietro Caraffa – a known and bitter foe of Spain – had gained the papal tiara as Paul IV, the French doubled their resolve and the conference rapidly broke down altogether. Ironically, after one further season of debilitating and inconclusive campaigning both sides concluded their own five-year peace at Vaucelles in February, 1556, without inviting England to participate. Mary's one attempt at European statesmanship thus rolled gently off the playing field, never to be seen again.

Prelude to war, 1556–7

Unfortunately, the Truce of Vaucelles proved short-lived, lasting little longer than it took for each side to replenish its treasury. It is still somewhat unclear what prompted Philip to provoke the resumption of hostilities by invading the Papal States in September, 1556. Perhaps the aged and cranky Pope Paul IV had provoked the attack himself in the hope of getting the French to drive Spanish forces out of his beloved Neapolitan homeland (**66**, p. 160). We do know that in a secret treaty of December, 1555, Paul promised control of Naples to the French if they would help drive out the Spaniards. Perhaps Philip felt the need to try his wings in war now that he had taken over the Spanish crown, and thus needed little prompting. In any event, when the Duke of Alva led Philip's troops into the Papal States in September, Henry II countered with his own force and the Truce came to an end.

Mary and her councillors watched this drift towards war with foreboding and dismay, for it placed England in a very tight position. While the marriage treaty had not committed Mary to lead her realm into a Spanish war, there were now enormous pressures brought upon her to do just that. Philip, who reappeared cap in hand after nearly two years' absence, wanted naval supplies, funds, and English naval support in the Channel, which was so crucial to the Spanish interests.

Mary and her councillors knew all too well the perils of granting such aid which would, in effect, have involved England in the war. Fiscal solvency would cease and popular support would wane even further at home, and there was quite enough to do in battling the remnants of Protestantism without the additional problems arising from Continental war. There were also some good reasons for not antagonising the French. Concern grew again for the dangers arising from French intervention not only in Scotland but in Ireland and the Pale of Calais as well. France was also an important trading partner. She absorbed a moderate but significant share of English wool and woollen cloth, and, in return, she supplied commodities which were not lightly to be sacrificed: salt from Bourgneuf Bay, sailcloth and other shipping supplies, and of course wine.

So long as Mary believed that France would take no hostile action toward her, she could accept the advice of most of her councillors and remain aloof from a continental campaign. Little by little, however, France played right into Spanish hands, dispelling Mary's hopes of maintaining her neutrality.

Right from the start of the English Protestant migration to the continent in 1554, Henri II had been sufficiently tolerant of English expatriates in his dominions to create some hostile reaction at Westminster. Mary and her councillors particularly resented Henri's decision to shelter some of the Dudley conspirators of early 1556. Later that year it was rumoured that he had designs on the Pale of Calais, with its garrisoned towns of Guisnes, Hammes, and Calais itself. Then in December, 1556, on what seemed a flimsy pretext, French officials confiscated a Plymouth merchant ship and held it for several months in the face of concerted diplomatic efforts to have it and its crew returned.

Finally, in late April, 1557, the English Protestant exile Thomas Stafford sailed from France on the *Fleur de Lys* in a hare-brained invasion scheme and landed in Scarborough. Though English levies brought his escapade to an end within a matter of days, this did not alter the fact that Stafford had sailed from a French port and had been supplied with French arms. When this news became known to the Privy Council the pacifists on that body could do little but bow to circumstance, and accept the inevitability of war (**66**).

Once the prospect of fighting the French came to be justified as a quasi-defensive or retaliatory measure, further reasons for such an undertaking began to emerge. After two disastrous harvest failures, which had allowed the conciliar 'doves', striving to avoid war, to argue about the state of the economy, the 1557 crops seemed well on the way to a bountiful harvest after good spring weather. From the standpoint of domestic politics a common enemy could be regarded as very useful in the task of reconciling a divided realm. In the event, a substantial number of those who emerged to lead England's forces on land and at sea had at one time or another opposed the regime or had been proscribed by it. These included the Protestant Earl of Bedford, who returned from exile abroad to assume command of the English contingent in the battle of St Quentin; Cuthbert Vaughan, Sir James Crofts and Sir Peter Carew, who had been implicated in Wyatt's Rising and saw such service as a means of reviving their fortunes; and the three surviving sons of the late Duke of Northumberland – Harry (who was to be killed at St Quentin), Ambrose and Robert, the future Earl of Leicester. In addition, war with France provided an excellent opportunity to paint with the brush of treason those English exiles who remained abroad (**66**).

Finally, England's military position had improved considerably at sea, and steps would soon be taken to improve her land forces as well. As recently as October, 1555, the Royal Navy had been able to provide only three out of a requested escort of fourteen first-class ships. From that point on, and with Philip's strenuous encouragement, the Marian government completely reorganised the administration and finances of its navy and undertook an extensive programme of rebuilding and repair. By the time of the official outbreak of war two years later, England could put twenty-one men-of-war to sea, with five more ships under repair in dry-dock and the five-hundred-ton *Lion* nearing completion. Command of the navy rested with Lord Howard of Effingham, whose son later led the English fleet against the Spanish Armada. Sir William Woodhouse of Norfolk, whose valuable service against the Channel pirates in recent years had gained him valuable experience, was appointed second in command (**70, 71, 66**).

Mary's council applied the same sort of administrative overhaul to the navy as it had to the customs system, and as it would later do to the land forces. Administration of naval finances was now placed under the jurisdiction of the Lord Treasurer – no doubt another idea of Winchester's, as well as an added burden for his shoulders – where it could be more closely related to financial administration in general. The council relied on the able Benjamin Gonson as Naval Treasurer, under Winchester, to preside over the £14,000 which was now allocated annually for naval operations. It appointed the equally able William Winter, whose career at sea was to blossom under Elizabeth, as Master of Naval Ordnance, a post which had been unfilled since 1553. Similar administrative rebuilding took place in the middle echelons of command. In the opinion of one modern authority, England's navy of 1557 was 'well led and better organized and managed than ever before in her history' (**70, 71**, p. 340). How ironic that Philip should have spurred on the very naval policy which served toward the undoing of his Invincible Armada thirty years later!

Mary's reign also marked a milestone in the organisation of England's land forces. By the time of the Anglo-French War, the traditional means of raising troops, through the feudal knight's service and the pre-feudal so-called 'national' system, had become obsolete: the former because of the transformation of the feudal context in which it had evolved, and the latter from disuse and disorganisation. Following close upon the heels of efforts taken to reduce exemptions from the obligation to do military service, Mary's last parliament passed the government measure known as the Militia Act. This began by acknowledging the disintegration of the quasi-feudal obligations for military service and placed the organisation of the 'national system' on a new footing. For the raising of troops this new militia counted on such officers as the Lord Lieutenants of the counties, JPs, and commissioners of muster. In some cases it relied as well upon the emergence of some stronger urban corporations as focal points of command, rather than expecting traditional landowners to call out their tenants – which was by now of limited effectiveness (**72, 97**).

The Anglo-French war, 1557–9

In late May, 1557, with the English hovering on the brink of war, the English ambassador in Rome reported serious rifts in the Franco-Papal alliance against Spain, and relayed the Pope's intention to sue for a separate peace. This relieved Mary of much of the discomfort of a war against the Papacy, whose authority she had worked so hard to restore at home. It may also have given the impression at Westminster that England could come in at the end of the Franco-Spanish fray, share in the spoils, and punish France for her impudence without much risk. With all these points in mind, the council acquiesced. Philip and Mary recalled their ambassador from Paris and on 7 June 1557, 'with trumpeter blowing, ten heralds of arms, with my Lord Mayor and Aldermen' in attendance, formally declared war against France: however the proclamation carefully avoided any reference to the Papacy [**doc. 11**].

The outcome of the war with France proved very different from what had been anticipated; indeed it is hard to think of any subsequent English campaign which has resulted in less material gain and more loss of face. The fall of Calais, and the tale of Mary recalling this 'at the bottom of her heart' as she lay on her deathbed, became familiar to generations of English schoolchildren. Yet this was not the whole story, and it would be misleading to perpetuate the traditionally narrow interpretation of the war.

Good → points In addition to providing considerable support to Philip's forces, the English role in the war effort consisted chiefly of four episodes: the work of the navy in the Channel and in the Atlantic; participation in the siege of St Quentin; the garrisoning of the Scottish border; and the defence of Calais. All but the last met with success.

In the months following the outbreak of war, the navy successfully cleared all French shipping out of the Channel, thus guarding

Philip's supply lines to the Low Countries. It carried the first English force, some seven thousand men under the Earl of Pembroke, across the Channel in July; performed valuable convoy duty for the Atlantic fishing fleet and the Spanish bullion fleet; escorted the Earl of Sussex to his Irish command; and, in the last important Anglo-Spanish victory of the war, used its artillery offshore to turn the tide of battle near Gravelines in July, 1558. Indeed, the achievements of the Marian navy marked the restoration of that strong maritime force which the Henricians had pioneered, and which the Elizabethans would employ so significantly (**71**).

English efforts on land met with mixed success. Some five thousand Englishmen joined with seventy thousand Spanish and Imperial troops in the successful assault on St Quentin in 1557. When Philip's forces broke through the French defences on 10 August he was determined to mollify his English critics by portraying the English role as crucial. In reality it was nothing of the sort, but the news of an 'English-led' victory aroused great joy at court and temporarily relieved the general gloom which had begun to settle around the Queen (**66**).

More decisive for English policy in the long run were the Scottish campaign and the battle for Calais. The first seems less an English victory than a Scottish defeat. Having rightly anticipated a Franco-Scottish invasion, the government prepared its defences with diligence. It was not surprised when, in October, 1557, the Scots marched south through Kelso and on towards the border. In the end they were defeated as much by appalling weather and dissension in their own ranks as by English resistance. The dissension arose between those who favoured the cause of the Catholic Regent, Mary of Guise, and wanted to maintain links with France, and those who tended toward Protestantism and thus remained cool to the whole idea of a French alliance. The rift eventually widened to the point of reversing the course of both Scottish religion and Scottish politics, though this did not come about until after Mary's death.

Had he been a seasoned officer, Philip would not have failed to press home his advantageous position in the autumn of 1557. With the Pope out of the fray, the French swept from the Channel, the Scots tripped up by their own swords and St Quentin in his hands, all of northern France appeared to lie open. Unaccountably, Philip called a halt for the winter so as to replenish his forces and his coffers; in so doing, he permitted the French to do the same. Determined to salvage something from a discouraging campaign, and fearing their inability to win much else before the necessity of suing for peace, the French found the garrisons of Calais an easy prize.

In a surprise expedition made even more improbable by the icy blasts of January, a large French force of some twenty-seven thousand men overwhelmed less than two thousand English and a few Spanish troops distributed among the three garrisons of the Pale. The defenders held out heroically for nearly three weeks, but with no reinforcements from either England or Spain – a factor which galled as much as the loss itself – the end was never in doubt.

The significance of this loss has long been debated. One view is that the fall of Calais delivered 'a crippling blow' to the Merchants of the Staple (**14**, p. 243). Yet the economic evidence, as discussed above in Chapter 7, suggests that this is a vast exaggeration: the French victory brought the Staple to an end more decisively but no more surely than the decline of traditional markets for English raw wool would have done.

How, then, do we account for the enormous importance attached to the loss of Calais by the Marians and by Mary herself; by the Elizabethans, who spoke passionately about winning it back; and even by modern history textbooks? Most probably, the loss of Calais represented a single, concrete and readily identifiable piece of evidence for the traditional case of England v. Habsburg Spain. That tradition, after all, was based on the belief that Spain pulled England into the war against her will, and it made much of the Spanish refusal (though not of the English failure) to rescue the besieged garrison.

A more balanced view, though not so nationalistic, would be that the loss was a severe blow to England's morale, rather than to her economic or military position, and that it came to symbolise everything which later Protestant regimes would see as wrong with ian England and its Spanish associations.

Ireland

In addition to participating in the high politics of European conflict and diplomacy, Mary also undertook two additional initiatives which remained important aspects of English foreign policy. The first was the search for new trade routes, discussed above. The second was a new departure in policy toward Ireland.

The English attitude towards Ireland at Mary's accession had many features which were to become part of England's imperial role during the subsequent three hundred years. Having been the dominant power in Ireland since Norman days, English regimes had managed to superimpose an English-style government over the parts of that island which they could control (the Pale) and made continuous efforts to suppress native interests outside that region. In the years prior to 1553 England had subdued the leading families of Leix and Offaly among other areas, but had not succeeded in finding a way to keep those lands, or indeed much of the rest of the English Pale, secure from incursion.

To solve this problem of control, Somerset's government had discussed in 1550 the concept of plantation, whereby settlers of proven loyalty would be sold confiscated lands and would move in to stabilise the area of settlement. Mary's government picked up this idea and set about establishing such a colony. The Crown surveyed the lands in question, divided them into manors as in England, let them out, and administered them under English common law and under much the same conditions as applied in English counties. The settlers were required to pay an annual sum to maintain roads and bridges, to provide military service of a predetermined type and duration, and to keep the peace. The responsibility for administering these plantations was bestowed upon Sir Thomas Ratcliffe, soon to come into the earldom of Sussex, who replaced the popular Anthony St Leger as Lord Deputy of Ireland in 1556.

Ratcliffe proved an extremely able administrator. With his brother Henry, he largely succeeded in establishing the plantations of Leix and Offaly, renamed Queen's and King's counties, between 1556 and 1563 (**74, 19**). The plantation system at its best still left some important things to be desired even from the English point of view. Its gains in administrative efficiency and in the establishment of law and order were qualified by its failure to deal with social and economic issues. Even the relative security it afforded was forever punctuated by native uprisings born of resentment and oppression. Yet we may still rightly consider this as England's first experience with several elements of colonial rule, from town planning to the administration of justice, which would be applied in the Empire of the future.

Compared to the substantial and enduring effects of the Marian initiatives in the plantation system, the reimposition of Roman Catholicism proved somewhat anticlimactic. Rather surprisingly, Mary's government does not seem to have pursued the restoration of the Catholic church in Ireland with anywhere near the same determination that it displayed in England. Several of the leading

Protestant churchmen, including the radical Bishop John Bale of Ossory, fled of their own accord at Mary's accession. The government took preliminary steps to deprive married clergy of their livings in 1554, and saw to the reconsecration of St Patrick's Cathedral in the same year. Yet even after Paul IV appointed Reginald Pole as Legate to Ireland in 1555 not much else was done for Catholicism, and Mary did not even return First Fruits and Tenths to the Church in Ireland until just a few months before her death (**19**).

This refusal to push too hard for the reinstitution of Catholicism in Ireland may be explained in part by the obvious fact that the majority of the population had never departed, as they had in England, from that traditional faith. Yet Mary's government also seems to have feared to over-emphasise support for what was in effect the faith of the subjugated natives in a colony where the secular governing authority had been associated with a Protestant ruling element for some two decades. In this case, at least, fear of civil unrest in Ireland, with the possibility of Scottish or French support, considerably tempered the official zeal for religious uniformity, and compelled respect for those in office despite their reformed religious views.

Summary

Traditional accounts of Marian England have too often presented the regime's foreign policy as a *danse macabre* to a Spanish tune. That tradition is especially vivid in relating England's involvement in the war with France and is taken to account for the loss of Calais. Even the development of the Irish plantation system has been viewed as an English adaptation of Spanish organisation in the New World. How does this tradition stand up?

In the effort to seek new trade routes the Marians displayed a necessary independence from Spain and showed themselves able to follow up earlier English initiatives to the advantage of the nation's commerce. In their Irish policy, too, the Marians seized upon and implemented earlier English ideas, and there is little evidence of any connection with the Spanish approach to colonisation. Yet in the main, Marian foreign policy must be evaluated in regard to its role in the high politics of Continental conflict.

There is no doubt that Philip went to great lengths to build up England's military capability, especially at sea, and that he brought considerable pressure to bear on England to enter the French war in 1557. Yet while he should be given the credit for much of the impressive naval rebuilding of the reign, the Queen and council seem to have resisted his blandishments to enter the war against France until they were convinced that such a course was appropriate for England's interests. Although the outcome of that fray was most unfortunate, this does not invalidate the reasons for entering it, especially when these are placed in the context of sixteenth-century statecraft.

Having involved England in war, Mary's government might have been able to use that situation as a rallying point to unify the nation. Certainly this started to happen when numerous former opponents of the regime rejoined its service in order to take up military commands. By the same token, English forces earned credit both for themselves and their country by their operations at sea and in the St Quentin campaign.

Yet Mary's regime failed to bring about such a rallying of national sentiment. One reason for this was that Mary herself died before the conflict could be resolved diplomatically. Thus she received blame for the loss of Calais but not credit for the peace which followed. She had no opportunity even to rally the nation around the symbol of defeat, as Elizabeth would do so well after the equally humiliating abandonment of New Haven (present-day Le Havre) in the French war of 1563.

For a nation which would undertake nearly a quarter of a century of conflict with Spain and an even longer struggle against the vestiges of English Catholicism, the apparent 'lessons' of Mary's pro-Spanish and pro-Catholic policies were too good an opportunity for the image-conscious Elizabethans to ignore. Taking their cue from such Marian exiles as John Knox, Christopher Goodman and John Ponet, and fortified by the carefully slanted view of Mary and her court, Elizabethan publicists like John Foxe portrayed Marian defeats as divinely-appointed punishments for a nation which had strayed from its intended English and Protestant path. To many Elizabethans, therefore, the defeat of the Spanish Armada thirty years later seemed no more than a proper retaliation for the wicked enticements of the Spanish King in the reign of Mary. By the same token the image of Catholics as somehow connected with foreign influence and political treachery became firmly rooted in the traditional interpretation of Mary's reign, the Spanish match, and the loss of Calais.

71

Part Three: Assessment

9   The Efficacy of Marian Government

Until very recently it has been assumed that Mary's regime, coming in the midst of what has been termed the 'mid-Tudor Crisis', found itself hard pressed even to manage the day-to-day business of government, much less to cope with the extreme duress of social and economic problems endemic to that era.

A. F. Pollard, the most prominent Tudor historian of the early twentieth century, played a considerable role in establishing this tradition of ineffective rule. In an oft-quoted passage written in 1910 Pollard concluded that 'sterility was the conclusive note' of the reign, and that '. . . in default of royal or ministerial leadership there could only be stagnation.' Pollard saw this stagnation arising in part from Mary's religious intolerance, but also from a fundamental absence of political leadership. Though he acknowledged the work of a few good men in her council, he found that most 'had no claim to their position beyond religious sympathy and the promptitude and energy with which they had espoused her cause. In their counsel there was little wisdom, and in their multitude, no safety.' (**49a**, p. 172).

Mary's parliaments, he felt, were wholly unsuccessful in their attempts to change distasteful royal policies or to modify royal intransigence in the face of economic and political crisis. Even Wyatt's Rising of 1554, militarily the most nearly successful of all the rebellions of the century, did not soften Mary to the wishes of her subjects as expressed by a frustrated parliament. Finally, Pollard claimed that Marian government suffered from what he termed an 'intellectual paralysis' which removed any possibility of sustaining the positive domestic legislation begun under Henry and advanced under the apparently benevolent rule of the Duke of Somerset (**49a**).

Though it should be clear from the analysis given in Part II above that Pollard's judgements must be qualified, they must not be taken lightly: they still describe the popular image of Mary's reign. Since so many of his aspersions were cast against specific institutions of Mary's government, it seems appropriate to discuss these institutions in turn as well as the issues with which they dealt.

The Privy Council

Much of the scorn with which Pollard treated Marian government fell upon the members of the Privy Council and on their operation as a governing body. He and most others who have considered the period have noted that the circumstances of Mary's accession impelled her to utilise appointment to the council as a reward for loyalty. Thus, they explain, the council became too large and faction-ridden to function effectively (**49a**, pp. 94–5; **26; 29**, p. 243). Yet, though the circumstances of Mary's accession had undeniable significance for the size and shape of the Marian Privy Council, the picture now seems more complex than has usually been assumed.

On the face of it, substantial evidence exists to sustain the conventional view. One might well divide most of Mary's councillors by background into two groups: those who had acquired experience of government in the reigns of Henry and Edward, and those inexperienced but loyal Catholics whom Mary could trust. In the same vein, a simple counting of those named to the council will produce the significantly large number that has supported charges of unwieldiness and factionalism.

Despite these appearances, however, closer investigation gives a different impression of the way in which the council actually operated. For one thing, the council seems rarely to have met with anywhere near its full nominal membership. A tabulation of average attendance would show its 'working size' as roughly equal to that maintained under Elizabeth: somewhere between ten and twenty councillors at each meeting. With few exceptions the Catholic backwoodsmen who enjoyed membership as a reward for loyalty almost never came: the remainder comprised a substantial pool of loyalty, experience, and – by Tudor standards – even skill (**98, 102**).

This effective separation of the sheep from the goats followed in part quite naturally from personal inclination, but it also received more formal impetus. In February, 1554, the councillors themselves set up a system of committees such as had been employed under Northumberland. Twelve committees, most of them apparently standing rather than *ad hoc*, were established in that month. They dealt with matters both routine and important, from naval administration and the collection of debts to the sale of crown lands and the establishment of a government programme for the coming parliament. Significantly they excluded the more casual councillors.

This arrangement took on a still more complex form at the initiative of Philip, who hoped to perpetuate strong conciliar government before his departure from England in 1555. Toward this end he helped establish a 'select' or 'inner' council consisting of nine of the most judicious and trustworthy councillors. In this group Bishop Stephen Gardiner of Winchester, the Lord Chancellor; Thomas Thirlby, Bishop of Ely; and Nicholas Heath, Archbishop of York, lent strong support from the episcopal bench. Sir Robert Rochester represented the Marian Catholic laymen and maintained links with the royal household. Sir William Petre, the Secretary, and Sir William Paget, together with the Earls of Arundel and Pembroke and the Marquis of Winchester, the gifted Lord Treasurer, provided considerable ability and little theological partisanship (**93**).

Though this inner council did not always function as well as Philip might have hoped, it did perpetuate and even strengthen the concept of conciliar committees. In the last and critical years of the reign the council set up *ad hoc* committees for such urgent issues as the conduct of the Anglo-French War and the management of finance: by then the system was well on its way to becoming a regular part of the council's operation.

There are further signs of institutional development in the Marian council. Partly again at Philip's initiative it played an important role in negotiating with Reginald Pole the terms of reconciliation with Rome. By 1555 the councillors felt the need for a corporate seal to enhance the council's authority, and one was introduced in 1556.

Still, there were undeniable rivalries among councillors, and the alleged friction between Gardiner and Paget is not unfounded. On one or two occasions it threatened to get out of hand or actually spilled over into other areas of government. Thus, for example, the impetus for creating the committee system in 1554 may well have come from Paget, who saw this diversification as a means of keeping Gardiner from controlling the whole council. Paget struck at Gardiner's influence again by urging the members of the House of Lords in the spring of 1554 to reject a bill for the revival of medieval heresy laws which Gardiner had sponsored. The House followed Paget's lead.

Despite these outward signs, however, there is little clear evidence of hardened factions lined up behind one or the other of these antagonists on more than separate and specific issues, and the council seems almost always to have been able to put personal rivalries aside at times of particular duress. Most probably, then, the Marian council proved less stultified by in-fighting, better organised, and certainly more able to administer than used to be thought.

More will be understood about the council's role in determining policy, as well as implementing its details, when consultative processes which went on outside the council become better known, especially those which took place in the royal household.

The royal household

Of all the central institutions comprising the Tudor system of government, least of all is known about the royal household. At its most familiar level the household did indeed look after the care, feeding and transport of the court. Yet one must now recognise that appointment to its upper echelons was the crown's way of keeping its most trusted servants and advisers – some of whom may also have served on the Privy Council – near at hand and accessible for consultation.

Office-holders who seemed to have little or no political function – the Master of the Horse, for instance, or the Groom of the Stole – in practice enjoyed almost constant and informal access to the monarch, and therefore had considerable power when it came to regulating access to the court for those outside its ranks. Undoubtedly all the Tudors were influenced to a considerable, though often indeterminate, degree by their household officers, and Mary – who trusted so few of her nominal Privy Councillors – may very likely have relied upon this inner coterie more than most.

Indeed, it would greatly facilitate our understanding both of Mary's policy and of the Privy Council's role if we knew more about the activities of such prominent household officers as Edward Waldegrave (Keeper of the Wardrobe); Henry Jerningham (Vice-Chamberlain); Edward Hastings of Loughborough (Master of the Horse to 1556 and Lord Chamberlain thereafter); the Earl of Arundel (Lord Steward), Thomas Cheyney and Robert Rochester (respectively Treasurer and Comptroller of the Household) and Henry Bedingfield (Vice-Chamberlain and Captain of the Guard from 1557).

Parliament

The historical literature on the history of parliament is undoubtedly richer by far than that on any other central government institution. The traditional approach to the role of parliament in the Tudor and Stuart periods was forged well back in the last century by the so-called Whig school of history. This put the emphasis on the growing initiative of the House of Commons over the House of Lords, and the attainment of parliamentary liberties against the authoritarian inclinations of the crown. None of the major twentieth-century proponents of this tradition had dealt particularly with the reign of Mary. Pollard developed most of his views on parliament by working on the reign of Henry VIII, while Sir John Neale wrote his classic studies on the parliaments (by which he really meant the House of Commons) of Elizabeth I (**45, 46**). Yet the traditions developed by these scholars certainly incorporated Mary's reign, and it is significant that no one of their generation felt inclined to spend more time on that 'interlude' itself. Yet in the past few years the close examination which has finally taken place has not only begun to undermine many of Neale's interpretations of the Elizabethan parliaments, but also his assumptions about the parliaments of Mary (**77, 99, 103**).

The first thing to notice about Mary's parliaments is the frequency with which they were held and the sheer quantity of legislation which issued from them. Mary called parliament in 1553 a few months after her accession, twice in 1554, once in 1555 and once in 1558. Although these assemblies were in session for a shorter cumulative duration than those of Edward, Mary's parliaments considered more bills and passed more acts per day of session than any others in the century.

Unfortunately this was not an inspired period for the keeping of parliamentary records: in neither Edward's nor Mary's reign were acts enrolled in the Court of Chancery as had been done under Henry VIII, and there are none of the numerous and enormously revealing private diaries which have illuminated the parliaments of Elizabeth or the early Stuarts. Nevertheless, a number of observations may still be made with confidence, based on materials which do survive.

In addition to calling her parliaments for the purpose of requesting financial appropriations, Mary followed the lead of her father and sought to gain parliamentary support for most important matters of state, including the religious settlement, the marriage treaty with Philip, and the conduct of the war with France. According to the Whig tradition, Mary's parliaments, dominated by the lower House, took strong exception to many of her policies, and particularly to those treating religion. In the words of the most recent comprehensive treatment of Mary's reign, Mary's parliaments 'foreshadowed the obstinancy of the 1620s' in their concerted opposition (**39**, p. 241). A closer examination of these views suggests some marked qualifications.

To begin with, it is known that Mary instructed her council to plan the government's programme prior to each session, thus assuring some orderly presentation of policy. Though a large number of bills were brought in by private members, either on their own behalf or on behalf of their constituencies, the government's bills were read first and enjoyed a vastly greater chance of being passed. This order of consideration was encouraged by the Speaker of the House of Commons, always nominated by the government through a member of the Privy Council sitting in the House, or by the Lord Chancellor (Gardiner and then Heath) who presided over the House of Lords (**96**).

In Mary's parliaments bills seem to have been introduced in roughly equal proportions in each House. Though the most vocal opposition came generally from the House of Commons, it should not be assumed that the Lords could be taken for granted by the government. For one thing, not all of the Lords were in agreement amongst themselves on many important bills, and the *Journal of the House of Lords* records on several occasions dissenting votes even on final reading. Secondly, the more active of the Lords frequently enjoyed influence on the Privy Council or elsewhere at court which was not the case with most members of the House of Commons. The Lords therefore had considerable opportunity to express opposition to government policies away from the floor of the House itself.

Contrary to what might be expected, religion does not appear to have been the only or even the most significant determinant of parliamentary opposition to the crown. Concern for the Reformation property settlement, whereby large amounts of ecclesiastical lands had been redistributed to secular owners, loomed just as large in the minds of those who sat in both houses of Mary's parliaments, and surfaced on several important issues. In the crucial third parliament of the reign, for example, neither House proceeded with the bill to reconcile England to the papal fold until an agreement seemed forthcoming which would confirm the current ownership of former church lands. In the same session the Lords rejected, at Paget's urging, a bill which would have revived the medieval statutes against heresy: they feared that it would again compromise the disposition of church lands. Finally, in the parliament of 1555, which was the most contentious of the reign, both Houses rejected a government bill to confiscate the estates of Protestant exiles (**77, 99**).

Somewhat surprisingly, the defence of the integrity of the crown and the succession also seems to have been an important concern in both Houses of parliament. Although they could hardly reject the treaty of marriage between Philip and Mary, both Lords and Commons, working together, effectively curtailed the potential extent of Philip's participation in English affairs. In 1554 they rejected a bill to include Philip in the protective clauses of the existing treason legislation, and in 1555 they prevented his coronation as King. Even in the wake of Wyatt's Rising, parliament rejected the crown's proposal to bar Elizabeth from the succession.

Thus far, then, it seems that Mary's parliaments were fully capable of standing up against what they regarded as undesirable royal policies, but the nature of that opposition is as important as its results. So far as is yet known, and with the possible exception of some debate in the contentious fourth parliament (1555), opposition seems to have arisen without apparent organisation or premeditated leadership. Critics of royal policies do not seem to have stuck together on more than one or two issues. Nor can opposition be correlated with specific religious convictions: Catholics as well as Protestants voted to oppose the revival of medieval heresy laws, to protect the distribution of church lands, and to preclude the coronation of Philip.

Finally, far from the cumulative opposition to royal policy growing snowball-like from session to session, which the traditional proponents of parliamentary conflict have assumed to be the case, Mary's parliaments seem to have expressed opposition in a spontaneous fashion. Members rarely spoke in terms of constitutional rights as was sometimes the case in Elizabethan and Jacobean parliaments, and whatever ill-feelings may have arisen in specific sessions do not seem to have been carried on into the next. The last of Mary's parliaments, convened in 1558 at the height of wartime distress, economic hardship and religious persecutions, was notably the most amicable (**77, 99**)!

In sum, then, Mary's parliaments do not seem to fit the assumed pattern of mounting conflict with the crown, of the increasing ascendancy of the lower House over the upper, of militant religious partisanship, or simply of more formalised factional organisation. They seem instead generally to have co-operated on most of the crown's policies, especially on matters of religion, and served as a willing partner in the passage of some important social and economic legislation. It must be said for Mary herself that she recognised in their number a majority of parliamentarians who remained open to compromise on most issues, and she was prepared to meet them half way. She thus did not press for Philip's coronation, despite his ardent desire to have it. She bowed to their desire to protect Elizabeth even in the face of some evidence that the latter had been implicated in Wyatt's Rising. She also graciously remitted a substantial sum which had been voted for her use in the 1555 session. These acts do not seem like angry reactions to parliamentary rebuffs, nor were they empty political gestures. On the contrary, they suggest a genuine spirit of compromise and co-operation which has not generally been observed either in the history of Tudor parliaments or of Mary's reign (**77**).

10 Mary's Reign in English History

Despite the relative administrative efficiency of Mary's council, the workable relations which she established with her parliaments and important government initiatives on several fronts, the final two years of the reign were dominated by a host of setbacks. The nation still suffered greatly from disease and the threat of famine. The persecution of Protestant diehards had reached an intolerable peak. The war with France had begun to sour and take its toll in men, money and morale. Against this background the Queen herself, never the picture of good health, declined into illness and prepared to die.

Mary's gynaecological history alone, including several false pregnancies and a probable hormonal imbalance which produced occasional bouts of hysteria, would have given any royal physician cause for concern. When she believed herself to be pregnant in March, 1558, Mary made out a will in which she bequeathed the throne to her first-born issue which, in the event of her death, was to be placed in Philip's care. Yet by mid-October she seems to have come to terms with her fate. 'Sicke and weake in body', she wrote a codicil in the knowledge that she would not bear a child after all [**doc. 12**]. Under the terms of the Succession Act of 1544 and according to her father's will, the crown was now to devolve to the Princess Elizabeth. A month later, on 17 November 1558, Mary died. The Roman Catholic regime which she had constructed and directed came to an abrupt end after a mere five years and four months.

It remains to ask whether, as some have had it, this was in fact a 'sterile interlude', an uncharacteristic and unproductive interruption of the apparently Protestant and 'liberal' course of English history, or whether Mary's reign holds some more distinctive part in that long story.

Certainly the popular image of Mary and her government tends even now to resemble the negative judgements passed by A. F. Pollard. Formed by the Elizabethans, who were anxious to justify Protestant uniformity and to rally national sentiment against the

Spanish and Catholic threat, and embellished by the Victorians, who were always anxious to stress the historical basis for English liberty, 'progress' and 'empire', that image presented Mary's reign as an object lesson in the dire perils of Catholic and authoritarian rule.

Though the superficiality of this view may already be apparent, it would be irresponsible to deny that it rests on a substantial basis in fact. All the more reason, then, to evaluate the significance of the Marian regime in all its parts, and to weigh it by impartial scholarly measures.

For a number of reasons, it is more difficult to arrive at informed judgements on Mary's reign than on most in the Tudor period. Chief among them is the brevity of the reign, and the proportionately high time and energy spent in establishing the regime and organising its followers. Because they broke sharply with their predecessors in foreign and religious affairs, Mary and her government faced a larger than usual task of political transition. Not only did they have to reward their followers and deal with their initial opponents, but they had substantially to reweave the whole political fabric of the nation: to stitch carefully together those personal links which attached the centre to the periphery and animated the administrative processes of shire, hundred and borough.

In some cases, though it was rarely so simple, this meant encouraging Catholic gentry families to reassert themselves in local offices and even in parliament, so that they might strengthen the new government at Westminster. Such transitional activity also meant more than the usual scramble for office and jockeying for position. The newly favoured were greater in number in this regime, and they took their time in securing their niches. Some of those who had been slow to support Mary strove to regain favour; others retired to a quiet life on their estates. A relatively small number fled abroad to await a more congenial government.

The most visible signs of this complex process came at the start of the reign: the forming of the Privy Council, the swelling of both the pardon rolls with those seeking exoneration and the ranks of the royal household with those rewarded. Yet these should not be taken to indicate that the task of forming the regime came to an end within a few months. It also entailed the replacement of Protestant JPs with Catholic, which took place to a significant extent in many shires (**88**, p. 303); the encouragement of Catholics to stand for election to some parliaments (**98**, pp. 15–18), the replacement of Protestant officials in the boroughs; and of course the large-scale replacement of Protestant by Catholic clergy. These were greater and more gradual processes in the creation of the Marian regime, and – especially in the last case – were by no means concluded even at its end. In the same vein, at least one borough (High Wycombe) received a charter of incorporation in return for its loyalty at Mary's accession as late as 1558, and not until the French war began in 1557 did numerous prominent opponents of the regime flock back to the colours.

In short, while there was considerable continuity in social and economic administration especially between the Marians and their predecessors, we must conclude that the process of shaping a distinctive Marian regime was still incomplete at Mary's death. This is hardly surprising, for it is now reckoned to have taken Elizabeth over ten years to accomplish the same task (**41**).

The short duration of the reign is important in the process of evaluation because so many of Mary's policies lay unfinished or unfulfilled at her death. Even in the opening months of her successor's regime her two greatest achievements – the alliance with Spain and the restoration of Roman Catholicism – were abandoned altogether. On the other hand, the search for new trade routes, the reform of the coinage, the increase in government support for measures of economic and social control and the revival of the navy were continued and brought to fruition only in Elizabeth's long reign. Ironically, many of these Marian legacies have been held up as unique accomplishments of Elizabethan rule, and have been used as points of contrast with the 'sterile' government of Mary.

In dwelling on the unfamiliar as well as the familiar aspects of Mary's reign, this book has in effect presented a revisionist approach to the subject. Yet care must be taken not to overstate that case. It would be wrong to overlook the deep religious divisions which Mary's policies exacerbated; to ignore the grave uncertainties about the future which plagued many of her subjects; to forget the intolerance and xenophobia which have left some traces to the present; or to gloss over the personal failings and misfortunes of the Queen herself. Though these factors have often been treated with emotional exaggeration, they are undeniably significant.

Yet when this has been said, one must still give the Marians their due. Indeed, it may not be too daring to suggest that the earlier initiatives of Thomas Cromwell's 'brains trust' and of the so-called 'Commonwealth men' of the 1540s – especially regarding administrative reorganisation, urban revitalisation, public relief and security from disorder – also remained active concerns under Mary. To these preoccupations, her government added its own distinctive policies in regard to finance, foreign trade, fiscal stability, military organisation and support for commerce and industry. Mary and her cohorts may therefore not have been doing so badly by the time their rule came to its abrupt and premature end.

Part Four: Documents

(*Note*: Spelling and punctuation have been modernised for the convenience of the reader).

document 1

Letter from Mary to the members of Edward VI's Privy Council, dated 9 July 1553 from Kenninghall

Considering the haste with which this must have been composed and copied, it is a well organised and prudent assertion of rights. Though not, technically speaking, a formal proclamation, the announcement of Mary's claim in this fashion did fulfil a formal necessity in the succession process. Copies of this letter survive in the archives of several towns to the present day, and must have been sent widely indeed as a means of soliciting support for Mary's cause.

My lords, we greet you well and have received sure advertisement that our dearest brother the King and late sovereign lord is departed to God. Marry, which news, how they be woeful unto our hearts, He wholly knoweth to whose will and pleasure we must and do humbly submit us and our will.

But in this lamentable case, that is to wit now after his departure and death, concerning the Crown and governance of this Realm of England with the title of France and all things thereunto belonging, what has been provided by act of Parliament and the testament and last will of our dear father – beside other circumstances advancing our right – the Realm know and all the world knoweth. The rolls and records appear by authority of the king our said father and the king our said brother and the subjects of this Realm, as we verily trust that there is no good true subject that is or can or will pretend to be ignorant hereof. And of our part, as God shall aid and strengthen us, we have ourselves caused and shall cause our right and title in this behalf to be published and proclaimed accordingly.

And, albeit this matter being so weighty, the manner seemeth strange that our said brother, dying upon Thursday at night last past, we hitherto had no knowledge from you thereof. Yet we considered your wisdoms and prudence to be such that having eftsoon among you debated, pondered, and well weighed this present case with our estate and your estate, the commonwealth, and all your honours, we shall and may conceive great hope and trust and much assurance in your loyalty and service, and that you will like noble men work the best.

Nevertheless, we are not ignorant of your consultations and provisions forcible, there with you assembled and prepared – by whom and to what end God and you know, and nature can but fear some evil. But be it that some consideration politic of some whatsoever reason hath hastily moved you thereto, yet doubt you not, my lords, we can take all these your doings in gracious part, being also right ready to remit and fully pardon the same freely, to eschew bloodshed and vengeance of those that can or will amend. Trusting also assuredly you will take and accept this grace and virtue in such good part as appeareth, and that we shall [not] be enforced to use the service of other our true subjects and friends which in this our just and rightful cause God, in whom our whole affiance is, shall send us.

Wherefore, my lords, we require you and charge you, for that our allegiance which you owe to God and us, that, for your honour and the surety of your persons, you employ your selves and forthwith upon receipt hereof cause our right and title to the Crown and government of this Realm to be proclaimed in our City of London and such other places as to your wisdoms shall seem good and as to this case appertaineth, not failing hereof, as our very trust is in you. And this letter signed with our hand shall be your sufficient warrant.

Given under our sign at our Manor of Kenninghall the 9 July 1553.

From Eye Borough Records, Suffolk Record Office, Ipswich, Ms. EE2/E/3, fol. 26v, reprinted by permission of the above.

document 2
Reply of the Privy Council to Mary Tudor, 9 July 1553

This negative response to Mary's letter – printed in document 1 – became the cause of considerable embarrassment within a few days, and its signatories would then claim that they had no choice at the time of its composition.

To my Lady Mary,

Madame, we have received your letter the ix of this instant declaring your supposed title which you judge yourself to have: the

Imperial Crown of this Realm and all the domaines thereunto belonging. Our answer whereof is to advise your forasmuch as our Sovereign Lady Queen Jane is after the death of our Sovereign Lord King Edward VI a prince of most noble memory, invested and possessed with right and just title in the Imperial Crown of this Realm, not only by good order of old ancient laws of this realm, but also by your late Sovereign Lord's letters patent signed with his own hand and sealed with the Great Seal of England in the presence of the most part of the nobles and councillors, judges, and diverse other grown and sage persons assenting and subscribing unto the same.

We must therefore (and of most duty and right we ought to) profess and declare unto you that . . . forasmuch as diverse divorces made between the King of most noble memory Henry VIII and the Lady Katherine your mother was necessary to be had, both by the everlasting law of God as also by the . . . laws and by the most part of the notable and learned universities of Christendom and confirmed also by the diverse acts of parliament removing it, therefore and thereby you made illegitimate and unheritable to the Imperial Crown of this Realm and the dominions and possessions of the same.

You will upon just consideration thereof and of diverse other causes lawful to be alleged for the same, and for the just inheritance of the right . . . and godly orders taken by the late King our Sovereign Lord Edward VI, and agreed unto by the noble and great personages aforesaid, cease by your pretense to vex and molest any of our Sovereign Lady Queen Jane's subjects, drawing them from the true faith and allegiance due unto Her Grace.

Assuring you that if you will for respect show yourself quit and obedient as you ought, you shall find us all and several [ready] to do you any service that we, with duty, may be glad with you to preserve the common state of this Realm, wherein you may otherwise be grievous unto us to yourself and to them. And thus we bid you most heartily well to fare, from the Tower of London the ix July, your ladyship's loving friends showing yourself an obedient subject.

(Signed) Thomas, Archbishop of Canterbury; the Bishop of Ely; Northumberland; Bedford; Suffolk; North; Arundel; Shrewsbury; Huntington; Pembroke; Clinton; Darcy; Mason; etc.

From Eye Borough Records, Suffolk Record Office, Ipswich, Ms. EE2/E/3, fol. 27r, reprinted by permission of the above.

document 3

The coronation of Queen Mary

It is interesting to note in this description the prominent place accorded by Mary to her half-sister Elizabeth and also to the unfortunate Ann of Cleves, another former consort of Henry VIII's who, like Mary's own mother, had suffered humiliation at his hands. The frequent appearance of foreigners here – the Genoese at Fenchurch and Peter the Dutchman among them – indicate the cosmopolitan nature of mid-Tudor London as well as the wide importance of the occasion.

The last of September Queen Mary rode through the city of London towards Westminster, sitting in a chariot of cloth of tissue, drawn with six horses all trapped with the like cloth of tissue. She sat in a gown of purple velvet, furred with powdered ermines; having on her head a caul [i.e. net cap] of cloth of tinsel, beset with pearl and stone, and above the same upon her head a round circlet of gold, beset so richly with precious stones that the value thereof was inestimable, the same caul and circle being so massive and ponderous that she was fain to bear up her head with her hand, and the canopy was born over her chariot. Before her rode a number of gentlemen and knights, then judges, then doctors, then bishops, then lords, then the council, after whom followed the knights of the Bath in their robes, the Bishop of Winchester Lord Chancellor, and the Marquis of Winchester Lord High Treasurer; next came the Duke of Norfolk and after him the Earl of Oxford, who bore the sword before her, the Mayor of London in a gown of crimson velvet bore the sceptre of gold.

After the Queen's chariot Sir Edward Hastings led her horse in his hand; then came another chariot having a covering of cloth of silver all white, and six horses trapped with the like. Therein sat the Lady Elizabeth, and the Lady Ann of Cleves, then ladies and gentlewomen riding on horses trapped with red velvet, and their gownes and kirtles likewise of red velvet. After them followed two other chariots covered with red satin, and the horses betrapped with the same and certain gentlewomen between every of the said chariots riding in crimson satin, their horses betrapped with the same. The number of gentlewomen so riding were six and forty, besides them in chariots.

At Fenchurch was a costly pageant made by the Genoese; at Gracechurch corner there was another pageant made by the Easterlings. At the upper end of Grace Street there was another pageant made by the Florentines very high, on the top whereof there stood four pictures, and in the midst of them and most high there stood an angel all in green, with a trumpet in his hand. And when the trumpeter (who stood secretly in the pageant) did sound his trumpet, the angel did put *his* trumpet to *his* mouth, as though it had been the same that had sounded, to the great marvelling of many ignorant persons. This pageant was made with three thoroughfares or gates. The conduit in Cornhill ran wine, and beneath the conduit a pageant made at the charges of the City, and another at the great conduit in Cheape, and a fountain by it running wine . . .

Another pageant at the little conduit in Cheape next to Paul's was made by the City, where the aldermen stood, and when the Queen came against them the Recorder made a short proposition to her, and then the Chamberlain presented to her in the name of the Mayor and the City a purse of cloth of gold and a thousand marks of gold in it. Then she rode forth and in Paul's churchyard against the school one Master Heywood sat in a pageant under a vine and made to her an oration in Latin and English.

Then there was one Peter, a Dutchman, that stood on the weathercock of Paul's steeple holding a streamer in his hand of five yards long, and waving thereof stood sometimes on the one foot and shook the other, and then kneeled on his knees, to the great marvel of all people.

Then there was a pageant made against the Dean of Paul's gate, where the choristers of Paul's played on the viols and sang. Ludgate was newly repaired, painted, and richly hung, with minstrels playing and singing there. There was another pageant at the conduit in Fleet Street, and the Temple Bar was newly painted and hung. And thus she passed to Whitehall at Westminster, where she took her leave of the Lord Mayor, giving him great thanks for his pains, and the City for their cost.

On the morrow, which was the first of October, the Queen went by water to the old Palace, and there remained till about eleven of the clock, and then went on foot . . . unto St Peter's church, where she was solemnly crowned and anointed by Stephen Gardiner, Bishop of Winchester (for the archbishops of Canterbury and York were then prisoners in the Tower), which coronation and other ceremonies and solemnities then used according to the old customs was not fully ended till it was nigh four of the clock . . .

From Holinshed's *Chronicles of England, Scotland, and Ireland*, 6 vols., London, 1808, IV, pp. 6–7.

document 4

The wedding of Mary and Philip

Though this was not published for some months after the event, it is clearly an eye-witness account. The plainness of Mary's ring, and the explanation for it, is more than a quaint touch: it tells us something about her essential innocence and simplicity of nature.

Then Wednesday, being St James's Day and the 25th of July, His Highness at 10 of the clock and his nobles before him went to the Cathedral Church [of Winchester] and remained there . . . until the Queen's Highness came, whose Majesty with all her Council and nobility before her came thither at half hour to eleven. And entering at the west door of the said Cathedral Church . . . Her Majesty ascended the foresaid steps and came toward the choir door, where a little without the same door was made a round mount of boards ascending also five steps above the scaffold. On which mount immediately after Her Majesty and the King were shriven [i.e. confessed] they were married by my lord the Bishop of Winchester, Lord Chancellor of England, Her Majesty standing on the right side of the said mount and the King on the left side.

And this marriage being ended and solemnized, which . . . was declared and done by the said Lord Chancellor both in Latin and in English, his Lordship also declared there that the Emperor's Majesty signed under his Imperial Seal the Kingdoms of Naples and Jerusalem to his son Philip, Prince of Spain, whereby it might well appear to all men that the Queen's Highness was then married not only to a Prince but also to a King.

The Queen's marriage ring was a plain hoop of gold without any stone in it, for that was her pleasure, because maidens were so married in old times.

This being done . . . the Earl of Derby before the Queen's Majesty and the Earl of Pembroke before the King's Highness did bear each of them a sword of honour. And so both their majesties entered the Choir hand in hand under a canopy borne by four knights towards the high altar, where – after they had kneeled a while with each of them a taper – they arose, and the Queen went to a seat . . . of the right hand of the altar and the King to another seat to the left hand and where they continued thus . . . their meditations and prayers until the gospel was said and then they came out and knelt all the high mass time, openly before the high altar . . . Where during the mass time the Queen's Chapel, matched with the Choir and the organs, used such sweet proportion of music and harmony as the like (I suppose) was never before invented or heard.

The High Mass being done . . . by my lord Bishop of Winchester [and] the Bishops of Durham, Ely, London, Lincoln and Chichester, the King of Heralds openly in preface of both their majesties and the whole audience so solemnly proclaimed this their new style and title in Latin, French and English.

. . . And thus shortly to conclude, there was for certain days after this most noble marriage such triumphing, banqueting, singing, masquing, and dancing as was never in England heretofore. Wherefore, to see the King's majesty and the Queen sitting under the cloth of state, in the hall where they dined, and also in the Chamber of presence at dancing time, where both their majesties danced, and also to behold the dukes and noble men of Spain dance with the fair ladies and most beautiful nymphs in England, it should seem to him to be another world.

From John Elder, *The Copie of a letter sent in to Scotlande* (1555). *S.T.C.* 7552.

document 5
Direction of Queen Mary to her council touching the reforming of the Church to the Roman religion

The following statement indicates Mary's good intentions, but also perhaps a hint of naivety: the restoration of Roman Catholicism entailed far more complex actions than seem to be called for here.

First, that such as had commission to talk with my Lord Cardinal [i.e. Pole] at his first coming touching the goods of the Church should have recourse to him at the least once in a week, not only for putting those matters in execution as may be before Parliament, but also to understand of him which ways might be best to bring to good effect those matters that have been begun concerning Religion, both touching good preachings. I wish that [they?] may supply and overcome the evil preaching in time past and also to make a sure provision that none evil books shall either be printed, bought, or sold, without just punishment therefore.

I think it should be well done that the universities and churches of this Realm should be visited by such persons as my Lord Cardinal, with the rest of you, may be well assured to be worthy and sufficient persons to make a true and just account thereof, remitting the choice of them to him, and you.

Touching punishment of heretics, we thinketh it ought to be done without rashness, not leaving in the meanwhile to do justice to such as by learning would seem to deceive the simple. And the rest so to be used that the people might well perceive them not to be condemned without just oration, whereby they shall both understand the truth and beware to do the like. And especially within London I would wish none to be burnt without some of the Council's presence and – both there and everywhere – good sermons at the same.

I verily believe that many benefices should not be in one man's hands, but after such sort as every priest might look to his own charge and remain resident there, whereby they should have but one bond to discharge toward God, whereas now they have many: which I take to be the cause that in most parts of this Realm there is over much want of good preachers, and such as should with their doctrine overcome the evil diligence of the abused preachers in the time of the schisms, not only by their preaching, but also by their good example, without which, in my opinion, their sermons shall not so much profit as I wish. And like as their good example on their behalf shall undoubtedly do much good, so I accept my self bound on my behalf also to show such example in encouraging and maintaining these persons well doing their duty, not forgetting in the mean while to correct and punish them which do the contrary, [so] that it may be evident to all in this realm how I discharge my conscience therein, and minister true justice in the doing.

From British Library, Harley Ms. 444, fols, 27–8, reprinted by kind permission of the British Library.

document 6
The report of Cardinal Pole's speech to both Houses of parliament offering to grant absolution to the realm, 28 November 1554

Pole arrived in England on the 24th of November, and delivered this address four days later to the meeting of both Houses of parliament, with Lord Chancellor Gardiner in the Speaker's chair. Pole begins by thanking Parliament for repealing the attainder which had been passed against him in Henry's reign, and then develops what has become a common Catholic explanation of the English Reformation: that a misguided monarch led his innocent people astray. This explanation implied no intended heresy in the realm at large, and made it easier for absolution to be granted.

In the first place, he returned the Queen and the Two Houses thanks for repealing the attainder, and restoring the privilege of appearing amongst them with safety and honour. After this, he entered upon the subject of his commission and acquainted them that, as they had been pleased to return him the advantages of his birthright, so his principal business was to restore the nation to its ancient nobility. To this purpose he had an authority from His Holiness to make them part of the Catholic Church. That the Apostolic See had a particular regard for this Island, and that to this, the Pope seemed to be led by the directions of Providence, which has given a preference to this country by making it one of the first provinces that received the Christian faith . . . To recount with what distinction and peculiarity of respect the English had been treated by the See of Rome would be too tedious an undertaking, neither should he mention the misfortunes which have pursued them since their defection.

If we enquire into the English revolt we shall find . . . avarice and sensuality the principal motives, and that was first started and carried on by the unbridled appetite and licentiousness of a single person. And though it was given out [that] there would be a vast accession of wealth to the public, yet this expectation dwindled to nothing. The crown was left in debt, and the subjects generally speaking more impoverished than ever. And as to religion, people were tied up to forms and hampered with penalties and, to speak plainly, there was more liberty of conscience in Turkey than in England.

. . . The Church of Rome might have recovered her jurisdiction by force, and had an offer of the greatest princes in Europe to assist her pretentions. However, she was willing to waive this advantage, and apply to none but friendly expedients. That, though the defection was general and strongly settled, yet the goodness of God interposed to our relief, and that at a time when it was least solicited and deserved. For when the true religion seemed wholly extinguished, when the churches were defaced, the altars thrown down, the holy ceremonies discharged and things brought to the point of despair, there were some reminders of the true faith. The Queen's Highness continued firm, to whom the saying of the Prophet may be applied without flattery: *ecce quasi derelicta.*

'Tis well worth our recollection to consider how wonderfully God has preserved Her Majesty. What contrivances were set on foot to defeat her succession? What numbers conspired against her? What preparations were furnished to destroy her? Yet, not withstanding the disadvantage of her sex, the surprise of the juncture, the inequality of her forces, she succeeded against her enemies and made her way to the throne. Now what can all this unexpected success be attributed to but the great goodness and protection of Almighty God?

From [the Apostolic See] I am sent hither, with the character of a legate, and have full powers in my commission. But notwithstanding my being entrusted with the keys, I am not in a condition to use them 'till some obstructions are removed on your part . . . My commission is not to pull down but to build; to reconcile, not to censure; to invite, but without compulsion. My business is not to proceed by way of retrospection, or to question things already settled. As for what passed, it shall be all over-looked and forgotten.

However, to qualify yourselves for this advantage, 'twill be necessary to repeal those laws which have broken the Catholic unity, and divided you from the society of the Church.

From Jeremy Collier, *An Ecclesiastical History of Great Britain*, 2 vols., London, 1708–1714, II, pp. 372–373.

document 7
The Injunctions of Archdeacon Nicholas Harpsfield on the condition of parish churches, 1557

As Archdeacon of Canterbury, Harpsfield was responsible for carrying out Cardinal Pole's injunctions for assessing and effecting repair of churches in the area of that archdeaconry. The following orders and observations underscore the sorry condition of the parish churches and the disappearance or decay of church furniture necessary for Catholic worship.

THE CHURCH OF GOODNESTONE

First, front cloths for the altar for the holidays and a canopy and veil against Lent.

The reparations as tiling and glasing to be done upon the Chancel at the said Michaelmas and the reparations needful to be done upon the church to be done at the said feast.

To make a new book of register for christenings and to be duly kept.

To make a new lock for the font.

Memorandum, that the vicarage house is in decay and that it may be considered how it should be repaired.

Memorandum, that the church yard is in great ruin and decay because it is taken to be parcel of the inheritance of Christopher Nevison it cannot be repaired. And yet the parishioners do promise to repair the same if they may enjoy it as their churchyard.

THE CHAPEL OF WELL, IN ICKHAM

Memorandum, that the Chapel is utterly decayed and that the tithes belonging to the said chapel are worth nearly ten pounds.

Memorandum, that there were two bells which are also taken away, by whom it is not certainly known but it is thought by Master Isaac.

THE PARISH CHURCH OF GOUDHURST

To provide a fair register book wherein they shall register all christenings, marriages and burials, and all the accounts of the church.

To provide two convenient banners before Rogation Week. To repair the chancel in sealing and other things before All Saints under pain of sequestration of the fruits.

To repair the glass windows of the church before All Saints.

Also, that the window in the belfry be glased before Midsummer, and to be closed otherwise decently (so that no pigeons may come into the church) before All Saints.

That the vicarage house be repaired in necessary reparations as tiling and otherwise before the feast of All Saints. And the same to be thoroughly repaired within this three years and the vicar to account what he doth bestow upon the same yearly.

That the churchyard be enclosed decently before Michaelmas and if it not be done then the churchwardens to certify in whose default it is the Tuesday after Michaelmas day at Canterbury.

From Rev. L. E. Whatmore, ed., *Archdeacon Harpsfield's Visitation, 1557*, Catholic Record Society, vol. 45 (1950) pp. 75–6 and 99; vol. 46 (1951) pp. 188–189, reprinted by kind permission of the Catholic Record Society.

document 8
The martyrdom of Dr Rowland Taylor of Hadleigh, Suffolk

The immediate cause of Taylor's sentence and execution was that he tried to prevent the Catholic mass from being celebrated in his parish church at Had-

leigh, on the Monday before Easter. Foxe, who was a remarkably accurate historian for the time, carefully recorded the entire episode, emphasising the expressions of public sympathy extended to this popular preacher, and sparing no details of the martyrdom being described.

When [Taylor in the company of the Sheriff and the latter's escort] were come to Hadleigh bridge, at the footbridge waited a poor man with five small children; who held up their hands, and he cried, 'O dear father and good shepherd, Dr Taylor, God help and succour thee as thou hast many a time succoured me and my poor children!' The streets of Hadleigh were beset on both sides . . . with the men and women of the town and country who waited to see and bless him. Coming against the alms-houses, which he well knew, he cast to the poor people money, some of which remained out of what had been given him in the time of his imprisonment . . .

His head had been notched and clipped as a man would clip a fool's, which cost the good Bishop Bonner had bestowed upon him. But when people saw his reverend and ancient face, with a long white beard, they burst out with weeping tears, and cried, saying 'God save thee, good Dr Taylor! . . .'

Dr Taylor, perceiving that he should not be suffered to speak, sat down. On seeing one named Soyce, he called to him and said, 'Soyce, I pray thee come and pull off my boots, and take them for thy labour; thou hast long looked for them, now take them.' Then he rode up, and put off his clothes unto his shirt, and gave them away. Which done, he said with a loud voice, 'Good people, I have taught you nothing but God's holy word, and those lessons that I have taken out of God's blessed book, the Holy Bible, and I am come hither this day to seal it with my blood.'

With that word Holmes, yeoman of the guard, who used Dr Taylor very cruelly all the way, gave him a heavy stroke upon the head, and said, 'Is that the keeping of thy promise of silence, thou heretic?' Then the doctor knelt down and prayed, and a poor woman that was among the people stepped in and prayed with him. When he had prayed, he went to the stake and kissed it, and set himself into a pitch-barrell which they had put for him to stand in, and stood with his back upright against the stake, with his hands folded together, and his eyes toward heaven, and continually prayed.

Then they bound him with the chains, and having set up the faggots, one Warwick cruelly cast a faggot at him, which struck him on his head and cut his face, so that the blood ran down. Then said Dr Taylor 'O friend, I have harm enough, what needed that?' ... At last they kindled the fire, and Dr Taylor, holding up both his hands called upon God and said, 'Merciful Father of Heaven! ... receive my soul into Thy hands!' So he stood still without either crying or moving with his hands folded together till Soyce with a halbert struck him on the head ... and the corpse fell down into the fire.

From Foxe's *Book of Martyrs* ('The Acts and Monuments'), ed. Rev. T. Pratt, Phildelphia, 1858, vol. II, pp. 351–352.

document 9

Excerpt from The Book of Rates of 1558

The following list of assessed items and their rates suggests something of the detail in which exports and imports were considered for this rating. Unfortunately, the 1558 Book does not list the unrevised assessment for our comparison.

Blankets called Paris mantles, red or coloured, the piece	xiii[s.]iiii[d.]
Blankets called Paris mantles, white, the piece	x[s.]
Bodkins, the thousand	xiii[s.]iiii[d.]
Bole Armoniack,[1] the hundred ...	xx[s.]
Boleus Armenus,[2] the pound	xii[d.]
Books, unbound, the half maund[3]	xl[s.]
Books, unbound the whole maund, xl reams	iiii[l.]
Boards for books called paste boards, the thousand	vi[s.]viii[d.]
Boards for barrells, the thousand	l[s.]
Boards for shoemakers, the piece	xii[d.]
Boras[4] the pound	xiii[s.]iiii[d.]
Bosses for bridles, the gross	x[s.]
Bottles of earth covered with wicker, the dozen	xx[d.]

[1] An astringent earth used as a styptic.
[2] A form of Bole Armioniack.
[3] A wicker basket used to ship books; usually holding 8 bales.
[4] Borax.

Bottles of glass covered, the dozen	xx^{s.}
Bottles of glass covered with leather and with vices,[1] the dozen	xxx^{s.}
Bottles of glass uncovered, the dozen	xviii^{d.}
Boultel[2] of Beaupre, the dozen pieces	xlviii^{s.}
Boultel called raines boultel the dozen pieces	xlviii^{s.}
Boultel called raines boultel the piece	iiii^{s.}
Boultel the bale containing xx pieces	iiii^{l.}
Bowstaves the bundle containing xvi staves	v^{s.}
Bowstaves the last containing xxiiiii bundels	vi^{l.}
Bowstaves the c containing vi.xx [6 × 20 or 120]	xl^{s.}

From T.S. Willan, ed., *A Tudor Book of Rates*, Manchester University Press, 1962, pp. 8–9.

document 10

Incorporation of the borough of High Wycombe, also known as Chipping Wycombe, by the Crown, 17 August 1558

The Charter here excerpted is a fine illustration of the full and detailed grants of incorporation which were employed with increasing frequency under Edward VI and Mary. In this case, the borough seems already to have exercised numerous privileges by earlier charters and custom. These are recognised and augmented here: the form of government is specified and its powers defined; the town's fiscal needs, economic activity, and public security are taken into account; and its citizens are granted certain exemptions from royal jurisdiction in those respects.

Whereas the town of Chipping Wycombe, *alias* Wycombe, co. Buckingham, both by charters ... as by custom from time immemorial is a free borough incorporate of a mayor, bailiffs and burgesses; ... and whereas the men of the town or borough have petitioned not only for confirmation of all their franchises and liberties but also for a new incorporation of the town and its inhabitants; In consideration of their fidelity especially in the times of the

---

[1] Blemishes.
[2] A kind of cloth.

97

rebellions of John, late Duke of Northumberland, and of Thomas Wyatt, Knight; CONFIRMATION to the mayor, bailiffs and burgesses of all liberties, franchises, etc. heretofore used by the burgesses and their predecessors.

And further grant that the said town of Wycombe be a free borough corporate of a mayor, two bailiffs and burgesses, and that the mayor, bailiffs and burgesses be a body corporate and politic and have a perpetual succession, that they be able to plead and be impleaded in all courts and places both spiritual and temporal in all actions and causes, ... and have a common seal ...

Twelve burgesses shall be called principal burgesses of the borough, every of them to be residing in the borough, and there shall be an officer who shall be called the steward of the borough . . .

Further grant of a court to be held before the mayor, bailiffs, and steward in the common hall called 'le Guildhall' every three weeks or oftener at their will with full power to hear and determine all pleas of debt, account, covenant, contract, trespass, force and arms, and other matters ... within the borough and its liberties not exceeding £20 in value ...

Grant of a weekly market on Friday and two yearly fairs to be held as aforesaid with court of piepowder,[1] stallage,[2] picage,[3] toll, fines and amercements and all other profits of the like markets and fairs; also of a prison or gaol in a convenient place within the borough ... ; view of frankpledge of all inhabitants and residents within the borough to be held twice a year in the guildhall ...

Grant of assize of bread,[4] wine and ale and other victuals and of weights and measures within the said metes and bounds. And power to the mayor, bailiffs and burgesses to make laws and ordinances from time to time for the governance of artificers and other inhabitants, for the victualling of the borough and for its better rule and governance.

The burgesses shall assemble every year on Thursday before Michelmas and shall elect a discreet and honest man of the inhabitants to be mayor for a whole year ensuing ...

There shall be two burgesses of parliament to be elected by the mayor, bailiffs and burgesses upon writ of election from the crown

---

[1]Court of pie powder: a court for fairs and markets.
[2]Stallage: a tax on market stalls.
[3]Picage: a tax for breaking ground to erect a stall.
[4]Assize of bread: an inspection of weight and quality.

and to be sent to parliament, there to stay during the time it shall be held, at their costs and charges.

The mayor for the time being to be a justice of the peace within the borough and to hear and determine there all things in like manner as the justices of the peace in the county . . .

The burgesses and men of the borough residing therein to be quit of pavage,[1] passage,[2] lastage,[3] tallage,[4] etc., throughout the realm; the mayor and etc., to have all manner of fines for trespass and other evil deeds . . . and issues and forfeitures of all men residing or staying in the borough . . . No residents of the borough to be brought before the king or queen's steward or marshal of the household for breaking the assise of bread, wine and ale or for any trespass . . . And no steward or marshal of the crown to enter the borough to perform his office except in default of the mayor and bailiffs.

From *Calendar of Patent Rolls, 5 and 6, Philip and Mary*, pp. 371–374.

document 11
The proclamation of war against France, issued 7 June 1557

Although the following was intended primarily as a declaration of war, it demonstrates a keen sense of propaganda in rehearsing the causes for such a declaration and, in fact, justifying such a step. The archives from which this is reprinted are those of the Spanish monarchy, now housed at Simancas.

Westminster, 7 June 1557

Although we, the Queen, when we first came to the throne, understood that the Duke of Northumberland's abominable treason had been abetted by Henry, the French King, and that since then his ministers had secretly favoured Wyatt's rebellion, acting contrary to the peace treaties existing between the two countries and to all honour, such was our care for the peace of Christendom and the repose of our subjects, that we attributed these doings to the French King's ministers rather than to his own will, hoping thus patiently to induce him to adopt a truly friendly attitude toward us. More, we undertook heavy expenditures to send our ambassadors to

---

[1]Pavage: a tax for upkeep of roads and highways.
[2]Passage: a toll on travellers.
[3]Lastage: a tax on market goods, measured 'by the last'.
[4]Tallage: a general tax levied on residents.

Calais to assist in peace negotiations between him and the Emperor; but our labours met with no return from the King. Lately, when Badely and Seaton started a new conspiracy, the King's ambassador was not only cognizant of it but received them in his house and supported them in their diabolical undertaking. Also, although the King had been fully informed by our ambassador of their doings, he received them at his Court and granted them pensions, disregarding the promise he had given an honourable person, acting on our behalf, and setting a very dangerous example to all princes, whose states cannot be secure if traitors are thus encouraged. He has also favoured pirates, enemies of Christendom, who have despoiled our subjects.

We realize that nothing we can do will induce the King to change his methods. The other day he sent Stafford with ships and supplies to seize our castle of Scarborough, not content with having intrigued so long with a view to getting possession of Calais and other places belonging to us across the seas and having financed counterfeiters and encouraged them to put false coin into circulation in this country.

For the above reasons, and because he has sent an army to invade Flanders, which we are under obligation to defend, we have seen fit to proclaim to our subjects that they are to consider the King of France as a public enemy to ourselves and to our nation, rather than suffer him to continue to deceive us under colour of friendship.

We therefore command all Englishmen to regard Henry, the French King, and his vassals as public enemies of this kingdom and to harm them wherever possible, abstaining from trading or any other business with them. Although the French King has molested our merchants and subjects, without declaring war, we have seen fit to allow his subjects and merchants forty days to leave this kingdom with such property as the law permits them to export.

From the *Calendar of State Papers Spanish, XIII, 1554–1558*, ed. Royal Tyler, HMSO, London, 1954, pp. 293–294.

document 12
The codicil of Mary Tudor's will, 18 October 1558

Written in the knowledge that Mary would not, after all, produce the heir she had anticipated and that she might not have long to live, this document is important for more than its role in the succession. It indicates the Queen's regard for Philip's power, her hope that the Catholic restoration might be perpetuated after her death, and the essential pathos of her condition.

This codicil [is] made by me, Mary, by the Grace of God Queen of England, Spain, France, . . . and lawful wife to the most noble and virtuous Prince Philip by the Grace of God King of the said realms and dominions . . ., the 18th day of October in the year of our Lord God 1558 . . . The which codicil I will and ordain should be added . . . unto my last will and testament, heretofore by me made and declared. And my mind and will is that the said codicil shall be accepted, taken and recognised as a part and parcel of my said last will and testament . . .

First, I the said Queen have, with good contentment and pleasure of my said most dear and well beloved husband the King's Majesty, devised and made the said last will and testament bearing date the 30th of March last past. And by the same, for that I then thought myself to be with child, did devise and dispose the Imperial Crown . . . unto the heirs, issues and fruits of my body begotten. And the government, order and rule of the said heir and issue I recommended to my said dear lord and husband during the minority of the said heirs according to the laws of the Realm.

Forasmuch as God hath hitherto sent me no fruit nor heir of my body, and it is only in His Most divine providence whether I shall have any or no, therefore . . . my said last will and testament which I trust is agreeable to God's laws and to the laws of this realm . . . And my debts principally I owe to many of God's subjects and the which they most lovingly lent unto me truly and justly answered and paid. I have thought it good, feeling myself presently sick and weak in body and yet of . . . perfect remembrance (our Lord be thanked) to all this unto my said testament and last will . . . if it shall please God to call me unto His mercy out of this transitory life without issue and heirs of my body lawfully begotten, then I most instantly desire . . . my next heir and successor by the laws and statutes of this Realm not only to permit and suffer the execution of my said testament and last will and . . . to perform the same, and to appoint unto them such persons . . . as shall be sufficient for the execution of my said testament and last will, and to aid them in performance of the same, but also if such assurances and conveyances as the law requires for the state of the lands which I have devised and appointed to the houses of religion and . . . to the hospital I would have erected be not sufficient and good in law by my said will, . . . I most heartily also require for God's sake and for the honour and love my said heirs and successors beareth unto me that my said heirs and successors will supply the imperfection of my said will and testament therein and accomplish and finish the same according to my true meaning and intent. For the doing whereof my said heirs and successors shall, I doubt not, be rewarded of God and avoid thereby His severe justice . . . against all such as be violators and breakers of wills and testaments.

And I leave and bequeath unto my said heirs and successors for a special legacy and bequest therein, I most heartily beseech our Lord the same may enjoy and possess, as I trust they shall, chiefly to the advancement of God's honour, and to the quietness of governance of the Realm, the which two things I most tender.

And albeit my most dear lord and husband shall for default of heirs of my body have no further government and order and rule within this Realm and the dominions thereunto belonging, yet I most humbly beseech His Majesty . . . to show himself as a father to his cure, as a brother or member of this Realm in his love and favours, and as a most assured and undoubted friend in his power and strength . . .

From Folger Shakespeare Library MS. X.d. 471, reprinted by permission of the Folger Shakespeare Library.

Genealogies

Table I

MARY TUDOR

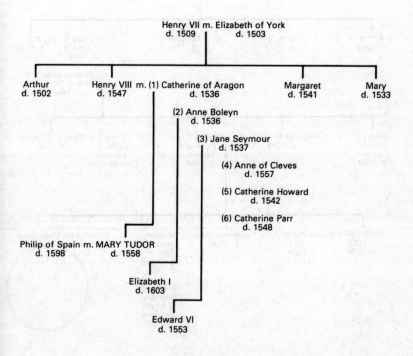

Henry VII m. Elizabeth of York
d. 1509   d. 1503

Arthur
d. 1502

Henry VIII m. (1) Catherine of Aragon
d. 1547   d. 1536

(2) Anne Boleyn
d. 1536

(3) Jane Seymour
d. 1537

(4) Anne of Cleves
d. 1557

(5) Catherine Howard
d. 1542

(6) Catherine Parr
d. 1548

Margaret
d. 1541

Mary
d. 1533

Philip of Spain m. MARY TUDOR
d. 1598   d. 1558

Elizabeth I
d. 1603

Edward VI
d. 1553

Table II

JANE GREY

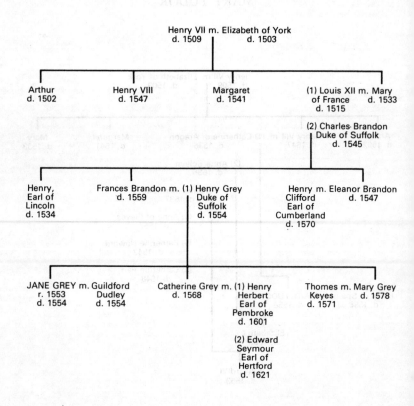

Henry VII m. Elizabeth of York
d. 1509   d. 1503

Arthur
d. 1502

Henry VIII
d. 1547

Margaret
d. 1541

(1) Louis XII m. Mary
of France   d. 1533
d. 1515

(2) Charles Brandon
Duke of Suffolk
d. 1545

Henry,
Earl of
Lincoln
d. 1534

Frances Brandon m. (1) Henry Grey
d. 1559   Duke of
Suffolk
d. 1554

Henry m. Eleanor Brandon
Clifford   d. 1547
Earl of
Cumberland
d. 1570

JANE GREY m. Guildford
r. 1553   Dudley
d. 1554   d. 1554

Catherine Grey m. (1) Henry
d. 1568   Herbert
Earl of
Pembroke
d. 1601

(2) Edward
Seymour
Earl of
Hertford
d. 1621

Thomes m. Mary Grey
Keyes   d. 1578
d. 1571

Table III

EDWARD COURTENAY

3RD EARL OF DEVON

The following table is intended to illustrate the Courtenay lineage which made Sir Edward the most logical English suitor for Mary's hand. Aside from his descent from Edward IV, his ties to the Blounts and Courtenays themselves linked him with supporters of both Lancastrians and Yorkists in the previous century. The following is not, of course, a complete record of these families.

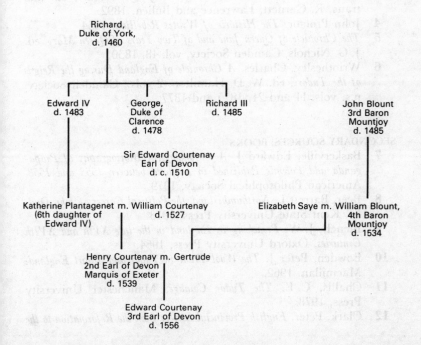

Richard,
Duke of York,
d. 1460

Edward IV
d. 1483

George,
Duke of
Clarence
d. 1478

Richard III
d. 1485

John Blount
3rd Baron
Mountjoy
d. 1485

Sir Edward Courtenay
Earl of Devon
d. c. 1510

Katherine Plantagenet m. William Courtenay
(6th daughter of   d. 1527
Edward IV)

Elizabeth Saye m. William Blount,
4th Baron
Mountjoy
d. 1534

Henry Courtenay m. Gertrude
2nd Earl of Devon
Marquis of Exeter
d. 1539

Edward Courtenay
3rd Earl of Devon
d. 1556

Bibliography

Note: The following list is selective rather than comprehensive. It identifies references made in the text and provides a guide to the chief works used in the preparation of this volume.

PRINTED PRIMARY SOURCES

1 *Chronicle of the Grey Friars of London*, ed. J. G. Nichols, Camden Society, vol. 53, 1852.
2 Foxe, John. *Acts and Monuments*, ed. Joseph Pratt, 8 vols., Religious Tract Society, 4th edn., 1877.
3 Guaras, Antonio de. *The Accession of Queen Mary*, ed. and trans. R. Garnett, Lawrence and Bullen, 1892.
4 John Proctor. *The Historie of Wyates Rebellion*, 1554.
5 *The Chronicle of Queen Jane and of Two Years of Queen Mary*, ed. J. G. Nichols, Camden Society, vol. 48, 1850.
6 Wriothesley, Charles. *A Chronicle of England During the Reigns of the Tudors*, ed. W. D. Hamilton. 2 vols., Camden Society, n.s. vols. 11 and 21, 1875 and 1877.

SECONDARY SOURCES: BOOKS

7 Baskerville, Edward J. *A Chronological Bibliography of Propaganda and Polemic Published in England between 1553 and 1558*, American Philosophical Society, 1979.
8 Beer, Barrett L. *Northumberland, the Political Career of John Dudley*, Kent State University Press, 1973.
9 Blench, J. W. *Preaching in England in the late XVth and XVIth Centuries*, Oxford University Press, 1964.
10 Bowden, Peter J. *The Wool Trade in Tudor and Stuart England*, Macmillan, 1962.
11 Challis, C. E. *The Tudor Coinage*, Manchester University Press, 1978.
12 Clark, Peter. *English Provincial Society from the Reformation to the*

Revolution: Religion, Politics and Society in Kent, 1500–1640, Harvester Press, 1977.

13 Cross, Claire. *Church and People, 1450–1660, the Triumph of the Laity in the English Church*, Harvester Press, 1976.

14 Crowson, P. S. *Tudor Foreign Policy*, Adam and Charles Black, 1973.

15 Davies, C. S. L. *Peace, Print & Protestantism, 1450–1558*, (Paladin History of England) Hart-Davis & MacGibbon, 1976.

16 Dickens. A. G. *The English Reformation*, rev. edn, Collins, 1967.

17 Dickens, A. G. *The Marian Reaction in the Diocese of York*, Borthwick Institute, St Anthony's Hall Publications, 1957.

18 Dietz, F. C. *English Government Finance, 1485–1558*, University of Illinois Press, 1921.

19 Edwards, R. Dudley. *Ireland in the Age of the Tudors*, Croom Helm, 1973.

20 Erickson, Carolly. *Bloody Mary*, Doubleday, 1978.

21 Fenlon, Dermot. *Heresy and Obedience in Tridentine Italy: Cardinal Pole and the Counter-Reformation*, Cambridge University Press, 1972.

22 Frere, W. H. *The Marian Reaction in its Relation to the English Clergy*, S.P.C.K., 1896.

23 Garrett, C. H. *The Marian Exiles*, Cambridge University Press, 1938, repr. 1966.

24 Haigh, Christopher. *Reformation and Resistance in Tudor Lancashire*, Cambridge University Press, 1975.

25 Haller, William. *Foxe's Book of Martyrs and the Elect Nation*, Cape, 1963.

26 Harbison, E. Harris. *Rival Ambassadors at the Court of Queen Mary*, Princeton University Press, 1940.

27 Hatcher, John. *Plague, Population and the English Economy, 1348–1530*, Macmillan, 1977.

28 Hoak, Dale E. *The King's Council in the Reign of Edward VI*, Cambridge Unversity Press, 1976.

29 Hoskins, W. G. *The Age of Plunder, the England of Henry VIII, 1500–1547*, Longman, 1976.

30 Hudson, W. S. *John Ponet, 1516?–1556, Advocate of Limited Monarchy*, University of Chicago Press, 1942.

31 Hurstfield, Joel. *The Queen's Wards, Wardship and Marriage under Elizabeth I*, Longmans Green, 1958.

32 Jones, Norman L. *Faith by Statute, Parliament and the Settlement of 1559*, Royal Historical Society, 1982.

33 Jones, W. R. D. *The Mid-Tudor Crisis, 1539–1563*, Macmillan, 1973.

34 Jordan, W. K. *Edward VI: The Young King*, Allen and Unwin, 1968.

35 Jordan, W. K. *Edward VI: The Threshold of Power*, Allen and Unwin, 1970.

36 Levine, Mortimer. *Tudor Dynastic Problems, 1460–1571*, Allen and Unwin, 1973.

37 Loades, D. M. *Politics and the Nation, 1450–1660*, Collins, 1973.

38 Loades, D. M. *The Oxford Martyrs*, Batsford, 1970.

39 Loades, D. M. *The Reign of Mary Tudor, Politics, Government and Religion in England, 1553–58*, Ernest Benn, 1979.

40 Loades, D. M. *Two Tudor Conspiracies*, Cambridge University Press, 1965.

41 MacCaffrey, Wallace. *The Shaping of the Elizabethan Regime*, Cape, 1969.

42 Maclure, Millar. *The Paul's Cross Sermons, 1534–1642*, University of Toronto Press, 1958.

43 Maltby, William S. *The Black Legend in England, the Development of Anti-Spanish Sentiment, 1558–1660*, Duke University Press, 1971.

44 Mattingly, Garrett. *Catherine of Aragon*, Little, Brown, 1941.

45 Neale, J.E. *Elizabeth I and Her Parliaments*, 2 vols., Cape, 1953 and 1957.

46 Neale, J. E. *The Elizabethan House of Commons*, Cape, 1934.

47 Outhwaite, R. B. *Inflation in Tudor and Stuart England*, Macmillan, 1969.

48 Palliser, D. M. *Tudor York*, Oxford University Press, 1979.

49 Phythian-Adams, Charles, *Desolation of a City: Coventry and the Urban Crisis of the Later Middle Ages*, Cambridge University Press, 1979.

49a Pollard, A. F. *A History of England from the Accession of Edward VI to the Death of Elizabeth*, Longmans Green, 1910.

50 Prescott, H. F. M. *Mary Tudor*, 2nd edn, Eyre and Spottiswoode, 1952.

51 Ramsay, G. D. *English Overseas Trade During the Centuries of Emergence*, Macmillan, 1957.

52 Ramsay, G. D. *The City of London in International Politics at the Accession of Elizabeth Tudor*, Manchester University Press, 1975.

53 Richardson, W. C. *Tudor Chamber Administration, 1485–1547*, Louisiana State University Press, 1952.

54 Scarisbrick, J. J. *Henry VIII*, Eyre and Spottiswoode, 1968.

55 Schenck, W. *Reginald Pole, Cardinal of England*, Longmans Green, 1950.

56 Smith, Lacey Baldwin. *Henry VIII, The Mask of Royalty*, Cape, 1971.

57 Strype, John. *Ecclesiastical Memorials*, 3 vols., Clarendon Press, 1882.

58 Wernham, R. B. *Before the Armada, The Growth of English Foreign Policy, 1485–1588*, Cape, 1966.

59 Willan, T. S. *A Tudor Book of Rates*, Manchester University Press, 1962.

60 Willan, T. S. *The Muscovy Merchants of 1555*, Manchester University Press, 1953, repr. 1973.

61 Williams, Penry. *The Tudor Regime*, Clarendon Press, 1979.

62 Youngs, F. A. *The Proclamations of the Tudor Queens*, Cambridge University Press, 1976.

SECONDARY SOURCES: ARTICLES AND ESSAYS

63 Alexander, Gina. 'Bonner and the Marian persecutions', *History*, 60 (1975).

64 Beales, A. C. F. 'Education under Mary Tudor', *The Month*, n.s., 13, vi (June 1955).

65 Blanchard, Ian. 'Population change, enclosure, and the early Tudor economy', *Economic History Review*, 2nd ser., XXIII, iii (1970).

66 Davies, C. S. L. 'England and the French war, 1557–9' in J. Loach and R. Tittler, eds., *The Mid-Tudor Polity, c. 1540–1560*, Macmillan, 1980.

67 Dietz, F. C. 'Elizabethan Customs administration', *English Historical Review*, 45 (1930).

68 Fisher, F. J. 'Commercial trends and policy in sixteenth century England', *Economic History Review*, X (1939–40).

69 Fisher, F. J. 'Influenza and inflation in Tudor England', *Economic History Review*, 2nd ser., XVIII, i (1965).

70 Glasgow, Tom, Jr. 'The maturing of naval administration, 1556–1564', *Mariner's Mirror*, 56 (1970).

71 Glasgow, Tom, Jr. 'The navy in Philip and Mary's war, 1557–1559', *Mariner's Mirror*, 53 (1967).

72 Goring, J. J. 'Social change and military decline in mid-Tudor England', *History*, 60 (June 1975).

73 Grieve, Hilda E. P. 'The deprived Marian clergy in Essex, 1553–1561', *Transactions of the Royal Historical Society*, 4th ser., XXII (1940).

74 Hayes-McCoy, G. A. 'Conciliation, coercion and the Protestant reformation, 1547–1571' in T. W. Moody, F. X. Martin and F. J. Byrne, eds., *A New History of Ireland*, vol. 3, Clarendon, 1976.

75 Heal, Felicity. 'Clerical tax collection under the Tudors: the influence of the reformation', in R. O'Day and F. Heal *Continuity and Change: personnel and administration of the Church of England, 1500–1642*, Leicester University Press, 1976.

76 Hurstfield, Joel. 'Corruption and reform under Edward VI and Mary: The example of wardship', *English Historical Review*, 48 (1953), repr. in *Freedom, Corruption and Government in Elizabethan England*, Cape, 1973.

77 Loach, Jennifer. 'Conservatism and consent in parliament, 1547–1559', in Loach and Tittler, *The Mid-Tudor Polity*, Macmillan, 1980.

78 Loach, Jennifer. 'Pamphlets and politics, 1553–1558', *Bulletin of the Institute of Historical Research*, 48 (1975).

79 Loades, D. M. 'The enforcement of reaction, 1553–1558', *Journal of Ecclesiastical History*, 16 (1965).

80 Loades, D. M. 'The Press under the early Tudors, a study of censorship and sedition', *Transactions of the Cambridge Bibliographic Society*, IV, i (1964).

81 Palliser, D. 'Dearth and disease in Staffordshire, 1540–1670' in C. W. Chalklin and M. A. Havinden, eds., *Rural Change and Urban Growth, 1500–1800, Essays in Honour of W. G. Hoskins*, Longman, 1974.

82 Palliser, D. M. 'The trade gilds of Tudor York' in P. Clark and P. Slack. eds., *Crisis and Order in English Towns, 1500–1700*, Routledge & Kegan Paul, 1972.

83 Pogson, Rex. 'Reginald Pole and the priorities of government in Mary Tudor's Church', *Historical Journal*, XXIII (1975).

84 Pogson, Rex. 'Revival and reform in Mary Tudor's Church: a question of money', *Journal of Ecclesiastical History*, XXV (1974).

85 Pogson, Rex. 'The legacy of schism: confusion, continuity and change in the Marian clergy', in Loach and Tittler, eds., *The Mid-Tudor Polity*, Macmillan, 1980.

86 Slack, Paul 'Mortality crisis and epidemic disease in England, 1485–1610', in C. Webster, ed., *Health, Medicine and*

     Mortality in the Sixteenth Century, Cambridge University Press, 1979.

87 Slack, Paul 'Social policy and the constraints of government, 1547–1558', in Loach and Tittler, eds., *The Mid-Tudor Polity*, Macmillan, 1980.

88 Smith, A. H. 'The personnel of the Commissions of the Peace, 1554–1564; a reconsideration', *Huntington Library Quarterly*, XXII, iv (August 1959).

89 Thirsk, Joan. 'Industries in the countryside' in F. J. Fisher, ed., *Essays in the Social and Economic History of Tudor and Stuart England*, Cambridge University Press, 1961.

90 Thorp, Malcolm R. 'Religion and the Wyatt Rebellion of 1554', *Church History*, 47 (1978).

91 Tittler, R. 'The emergence of urban policy, 1536–1558' in Loach and Tittler, eds., *The Mid-Tudor Polity*, Macmillan, 1980.

92 Tittler, R. 'The incorporation of boroughs, 1540–1558', *History*, 62, no. 204 (Feb. 1977).

93 Weikel, A. 'The Marian council revisited' in Loach and Tittler, eds., *The Mid-Tudor Polity*, Macmillan, 1980.

SECONDARY SOURCES: UNPUBLISHED THESES

94 Bartholomew, Alison, 'Lay piety in the reign of Mary Tudor', Manchester MA, 1979.

95 Dawson, Jane E. A. 'The early career of Christopher Goodman and his place in the development of English Protestant thought', Durham PhD, 1978.

96 Ericson, C. G. 'Parliament as a legislative institution in the reigns of Edward VI and Mary', London PhD, 1974.

97 Goring, John Jeremy. 'The military obligations of the English people, 1511–1558', London PhD, 1955.

98 Lemasters, G. E. 'The Privy Council in the reign of Queen Mary I', Cambridge PhD, 1972.

99 Loach, S. J. 'Opposition to the crown in parliament, 1553–1558', Oxford D Phil, 1974.

100 Smith, Patricia. 'The brewing industry in Tudor England', Concordia MA, 1981.

101 Took, Patricia M. 'The government and the printing trade, 1540–1560', London PhD, 1979.

102 Weikel, Ann. 'Crown and council; a study of Mary Tudor and her Privy Council', Yale PhD, 1966.

Bibliography

ADDENDA

103 Graves, Michael A. R. *The House of Lords in the Parliaments of Edward VI and Mary*, Cambridge University Press, 1981.

104 Martin, J. W. 'Miles Hogarde: artisan and aspiring author in sixteenth century England', *Renaissance Quarterly*, XXXIV, no. 3 (1981).

105 Martin, J. W. 'The Marian regime's failure to understand the importance of printing', *Huntington Library Quarterly*, in press.

106 Bartlett, Kenneth R. 'The english exile community in Italy and the political opposition to Mary I', *Albion*, XIII, no. 3 (1981).

Index

Index

Cornish Rising (1497), 59
Cotswolds, 10
Courtenay, Edward, *see* Devon, earl of
Coventry, 4
Cranbrook, Kent, 19
Cranmer, Thomas, Archbishop, 25, 27, 28, 40, 47, 86
Crofts, James, 64
Cromwell, Thomas, 40, 47, 58, 82
customs, 4, 53–5, 59, 96–7

Derby, (Edward Stanley), earl of, 89
Devon, (Edward Courtenay), earl of, 16–17, 18, 19, 105
Dominican Order, 28–9
Dudley, Ambrose, 64
Dudley, Guildford, 8, 104
Dudley, Harry, 64
Dudley, John, *see* Northumberland
Dudley, Robert, 10, 64
Dudley Conspiracy, 64
Durham, bishopric of, 25

Eastland Company, 52
economic policy, 14, 50–60, 82
education, 33, 57; *see also* Oxford University, Cambridge University
Edward VI, 25, 84–6, 103; birth, 2, 3, 5; death, 8–9, 11, 84
Elizabeth, Princess, 2, 18, 19, 20, 78–9, 80, 87, 103; reign of, 35, 37–8, 44, 45, 48, 54, 55–6, 57–8, 59, 67, 68, 76, 80, 82
Elizabethan Settlement, 38
Elton, Professor G.R., 40
Emden, 36
Englefield, Francis, 13, 54
Erasmus of Rotterdam, 48
Exchequer, Court of, 55, 58
explorations, 50–1, 52, 68, 82

finance, government, 4, 53–5, 58, 59, 63, 74, 83
First Fruits and Tenths, Court of, 58
Fitzroy, Henry, 1
foreign affairs, 14, 16, 61–71, *see* war
Foxe, John, 35–6, 71
Framlingham, Suffolk, 11
France, 16, 36, 46, 50, 61–71, 99–100; *see* War, Anglo-French
Frankfurt, 36, 41, 43

Gardiner, Stephen, Bishop of Winchester, Lord Chancellor, 13, 16, 17, 33, 38, 46, 74, 77, 87, 88–90
Garrett, Christina, 36
Geneva, 36, 37, 41, 43–4
gilds, 4, 5, 55–56
Gonson, Benjamin, 65
Goodman, Christopher, 43, 44, 45, 71
Goodnestone, Kent, 93–4
Goudhurst, Kent, 94
grain, 57
Gravelines, Battle of (1558), 67
Great Yarmouth, Norf., 9, 10, 12
Greenwich, 9
Guinea, 52
Gwynneth, John, 46

Habsburgs, 3, 16, 61–2; *see also* Charles V, Philip
Hadleigh, Suffolk, 34, 94–6
Hanseatic League, 50
Harpsfield, John, 47
Harpsfield, Nicholas, 46, 93–4
Hastings, (Edward) baron of Loughborough, 11, 75, 87
Heath, Nicholas, Archbishop and Lord Chancellor, 74, 77
Henry II, king of France, 63–4, 99–100
Henry VII, 53, 103, 104
Henry VIII, 1, 2, 5, 16, 23, 25, 29, 30, 31, 40, 59, 67, 72, 73, 76, 103, 104; will of, 2, 80, 84–5
Higham Ferrars, Northants., 10
High Wycombe, Bucks., 10, 82, 97–9
Hoddesdon, Herts., 9
Household, the Royal, 13, 75, 81
Howard, (William) baron of Effingham, Lord Admiral, 65
Huddleston, John, 9
Huggard (or Hogarde), Miles, 38, 46

Ickham, Kent, 94
impositions, 54–5
inflation, 54
industry, 4, 50, 54, 55–6, 83
Ireland, 63, 67, 68–70
Italy, 61; *see also* Milan, Padua, Papacy

James V, king of Scotland, 61
Jane Grey, 8, 10–11, 12, 19, 20, 86, 104
Jane Seymour, 2, 103

114